Sheree Hovsepian

jrp|editions

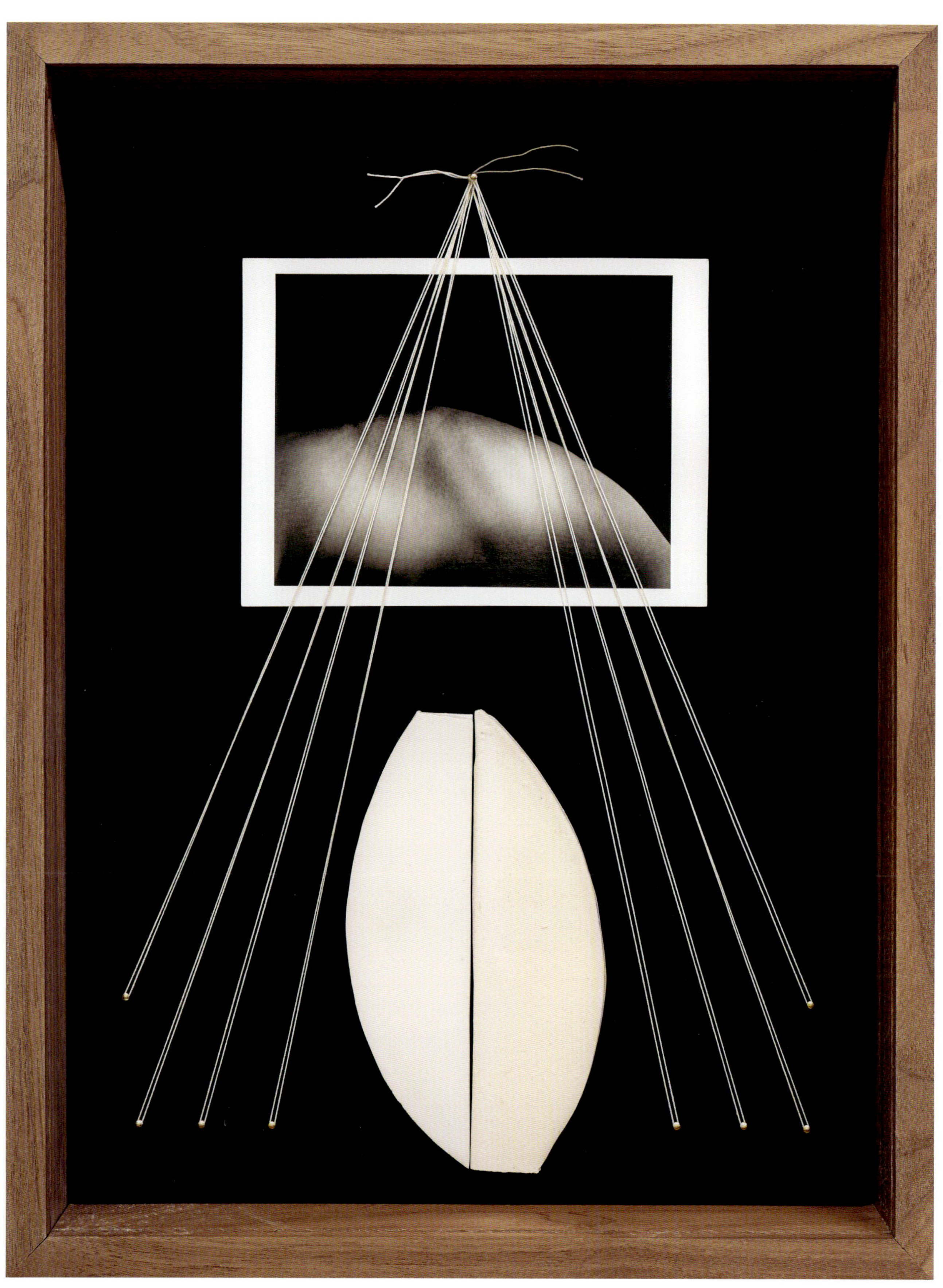

Lucida, 2020

Charlotte Cotton

Each experience of Sheree Hovsepian's individual works and exhibition installations brings our attention to the multivalent ways in which she constellates, refines, and abstracts the labors of a daily studio-based practice. Multiple materials are rendered into interconnecting forms and gestures. Found objects are corralled. Photographs act as pivots in these bodily constructions, with each element garnered from her highly sensitized, haptic forms of art making. This book draws together a selection of work made by Hovsepian since 2012, and gives an animated unfolding of the adjacencies and contrasts of her principal bodies of work, and her ongoing material experiments.

The earliest works shown here are grouped under the titles *Material Gestures* (2012–ongoing; p. 40–42), *Haptic Wonders* (2012; p. 51–53), and *Sleight of Hand* (2013; p. 34–39), which directly entreat us to pay close attention to the physicality of Hovsepian's work and its making. *Material Gestures* are wall-based arrangements of stretched fabric and string nailed into geometric formations, asymmetrical and evidently hand-crafted porcelain tiles, and analog black and white photographs of a human female form. All of these mediumistic elements would become the recurring vocabulary of the artist's assemblage works over the coming years, along with other materials such as fleshy stretched nylon, and wood found on the way to her studio that she whittles into limb-like shapes for her constructions. Her cache of printed photographs—camera-less and abstract traces of her performative studio practices; curled, collaged, and sculptural photographic objects; and the capture of her most figurative work such as *Leaning* (2019; p. 47–49) where her sister enacts the role of stand-in subject for Hovsepian— are often the spines and hearts of these exquisite corpse assemblages.

Haptic Wonders is a large series of striking photograms—the enduringly experimental, camera-less process that staccatos throughout the history of analog photography—recording sequences of the artist's movements. These photographs index her manual processes of masking and exposing, and the cutting out and layering of silhouettes directly onto light-sensitive paper in the confines of a darkroom, using her cell phone as a light source. For Hovsepian, this is a physical and intellectual process of distilling the movements of her body and finding abstract compositions within the resulting mark making. This elemental nature of photograms has been a practice through which she has learned and experimented with making abstract gestures and embracing the unique and wonderful happenstance of combining light, darkness, chemical reactions, and the haptic movements of her body.

For her *Sleight of Hand* monochromes in black, red, blue, and purple, she captures each series of consequential actions in her studio environment within one image. Using an analog film camera, she makes multiple exposures of sheets of paper arranged in lines and fanned onto a studio wall, removing the arrangement sheet-by-sheet as she photographs from a fixed (yet subtly oscillating) vantage point. In this minimalistic gesture of adding multiple exposures while removing the sheets of paper from the wall, she intentionally builds up the "in-camera" indexing of the layering presence and absence. Within the context of this foundational body of work, photography manifests as an additive process and Hovsepian consciously relates these photographic actions to those of painting. The effect of Color Field painting of the mid-20th century is embedded in the framing strategy that she is using in *Sleight of Hand*, where the studio wall and floor is visible, and forms the compositional structure within the final frame. This contextualizing device refers to the grounding within abstract paintings that horizon lines provide, as well as supplying a sense of scale of the artist's studio work, and the time and place of its making.

The haptic nature of mark and art making, and the animated celebration of the sorts of properties and possibilities of analog mediums is a continuing throughline in Hovsepian's practice. This is evident in her 2022 *Muscle Memory* (p. 32–33) series of large, part-abstract part-figurative, ink drawings made in her studio by syringing the ink onto the paper, which she simply lifts and tilts to influence the direction of the ink's flow before it dries. These performative and durational works may use different materials than, for example, her camera-less photographs, but they similarly hinge upon the combined behavior of the medium and the movements of her body. They provide a bodily affect to the viewer, where we read the artist's gestures.

 The shared characteristics of processes and tools that Hovsepian puts into play is not an amplified critique of traditional modernist hierarchies of art mediums, yet it is a flattening of them. Within the historic pyramid of value, painting and sculpture are placed above drawing and photography, which in turn may be positioned above ceramics, fiber art, and woodwork. Hovsepian manifests a deep love of these traditional mediums as the genuine and experimental tools of her practice that she interconnects through their non-hierarchical equivalency with each other. It is part of the disarming effect within her small sculptures made from cast bronze—a symbolically loaded material within the history of art (p. 28). Her bronzes are delicate and idiosyncratically rendered by hand, shifting between abstract and figurative readings. They are as modest and humble as a human limb, as touching as the webs of string macramé stretched and nailed into her assemblage works that honor her own mother's handicraft making that inspired her while growing up. The shape and surface reticulations of the bronzes are facsimiles of the soft wax models that she crafts, and from which the bronzes' molds are made. Within the context of her practice, the positive (wax) and negative (mold) casting stages can be read as akin to the analog photography negative-to-positive process, and of no more than equal value.

 Hovsepian's analog referencing and thinking in a digital era are deliberate strategies for holding the attention of viewers. By manifesting materials in unexpected and abstracting ways, our attention is held as we attempt to figure out the meaning and value of these no-longer-default techniques and rendering technologies. In her own way, she beautifully lays out works and installations that are rendered from a sequence of active and idiosyncratic choices and determined gestures that are simultaneously photographic, sculptural, and painterly, liberated from the bounds of time, within the flattened hierarchy of contemporary creative roles and identities. We see this manifest in individual assemblages and the ways in which we can readily connect the multiple materials and their conditional meanings as a constellated whole. We similarly experience these parities in the placement of works—and the contingency between them—in her exhibition installations. Hovsepian orchestrates these bodily experiences for us to be in direct and physical proximity to both her making processes and the contemplative, experimental space of her studio. She invites us to look deeply, and in the ways in which a studio practice transitions into a gallery context, and into the space of shared, material consideration.

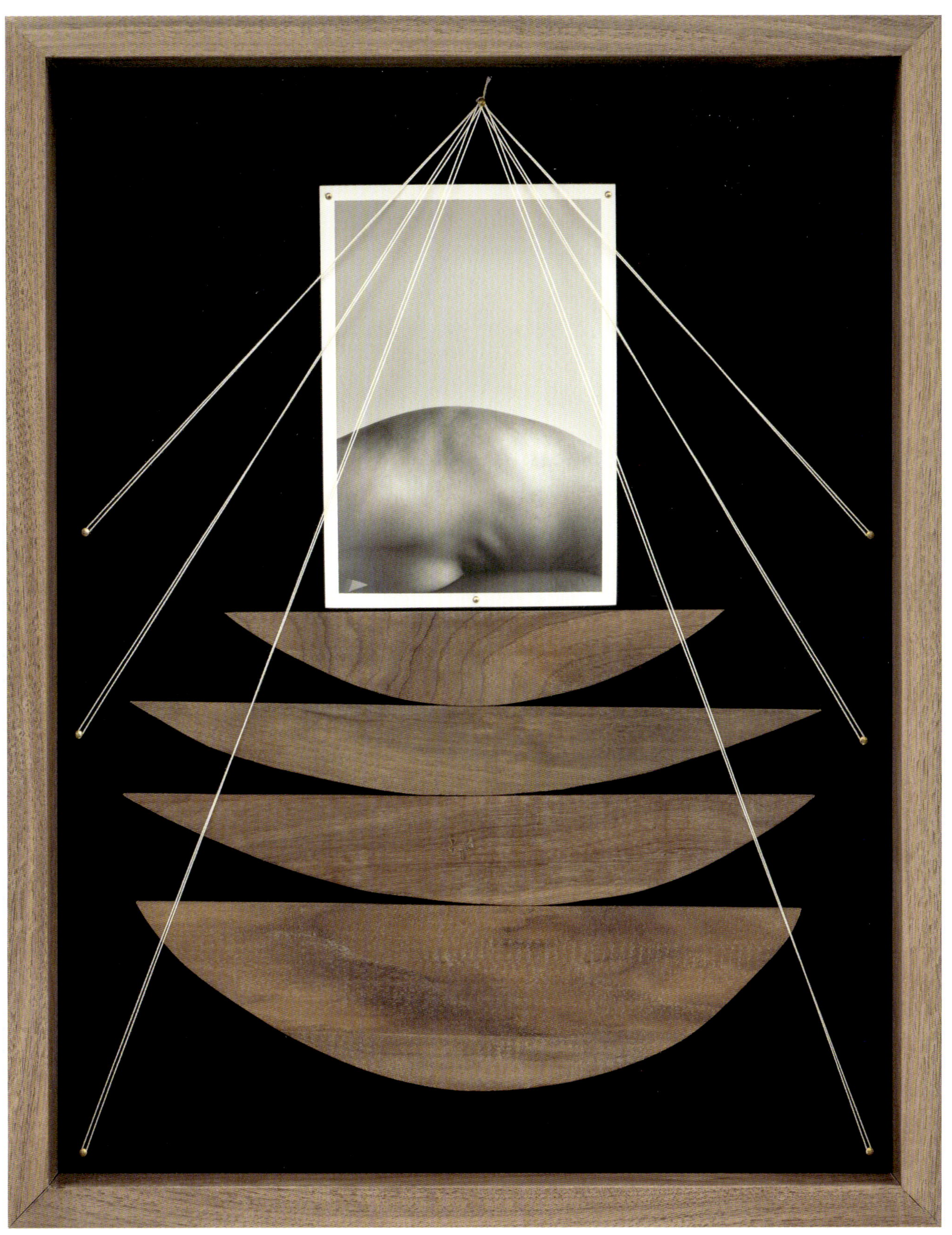

Euclidean Space, 2022

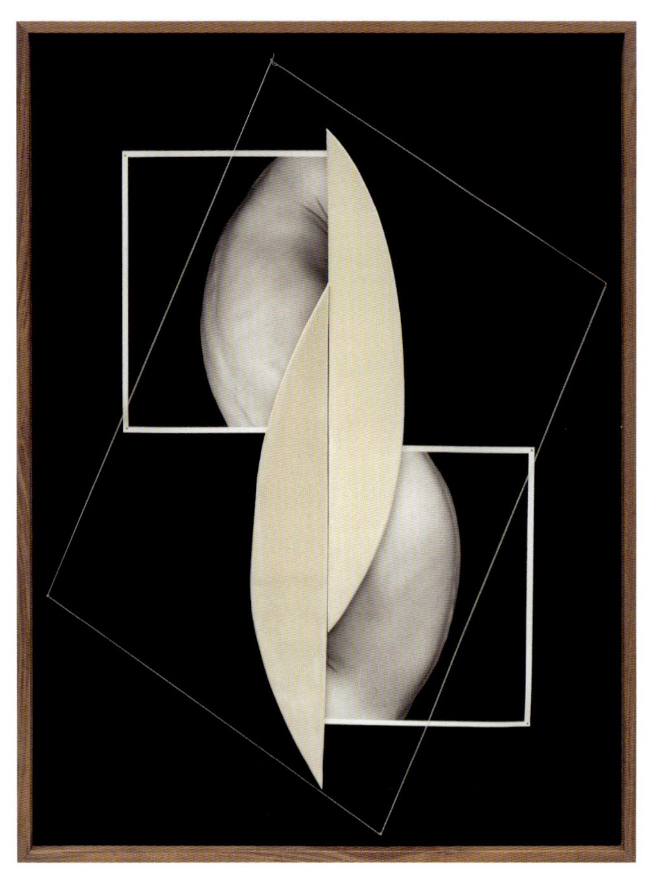

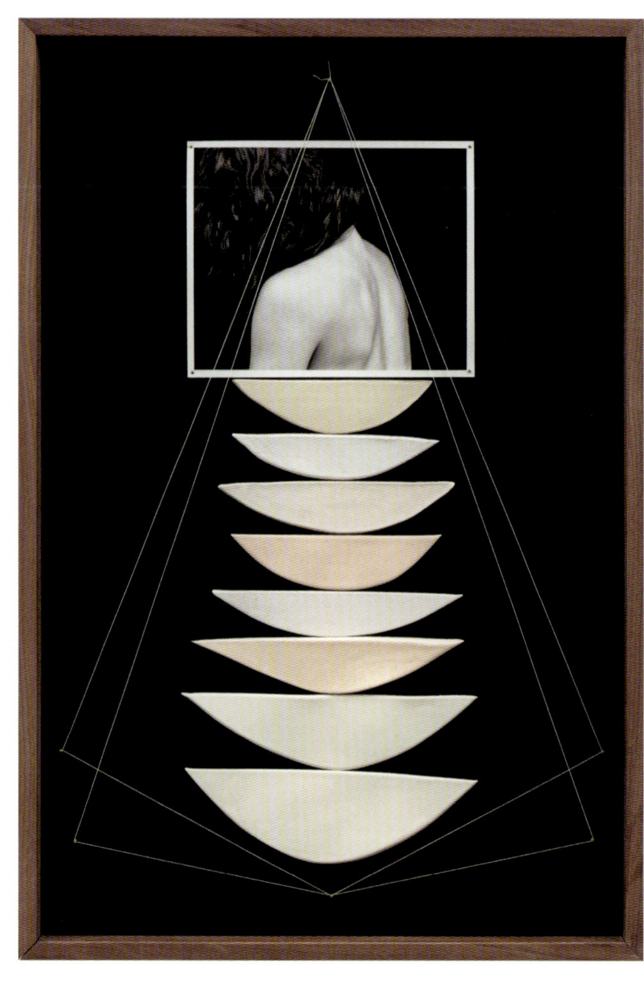

Acolyte, 2023
Relic, 2022

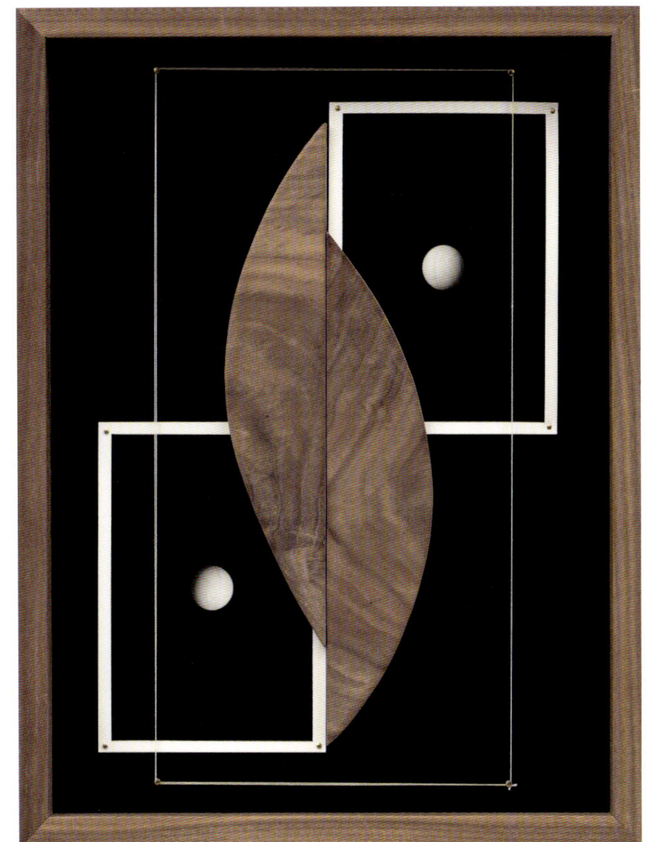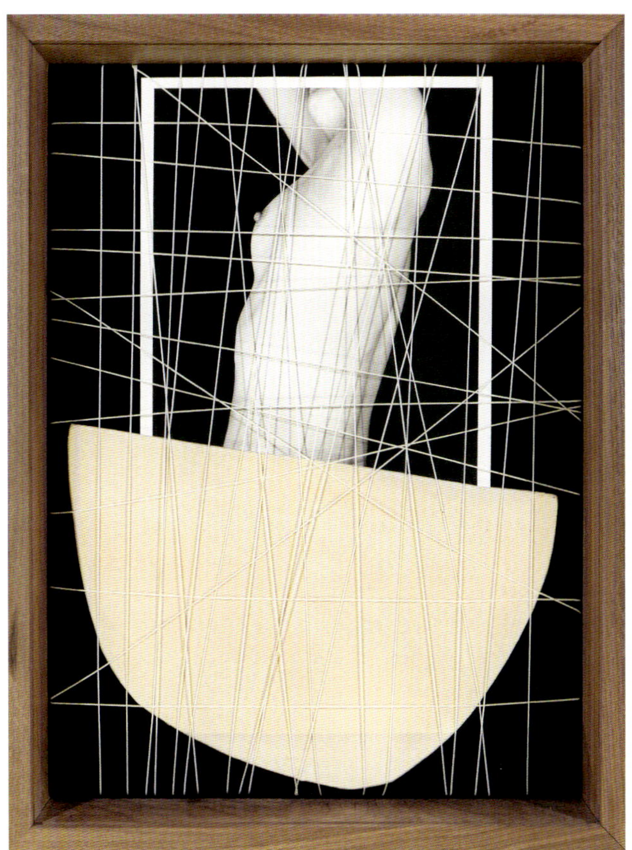

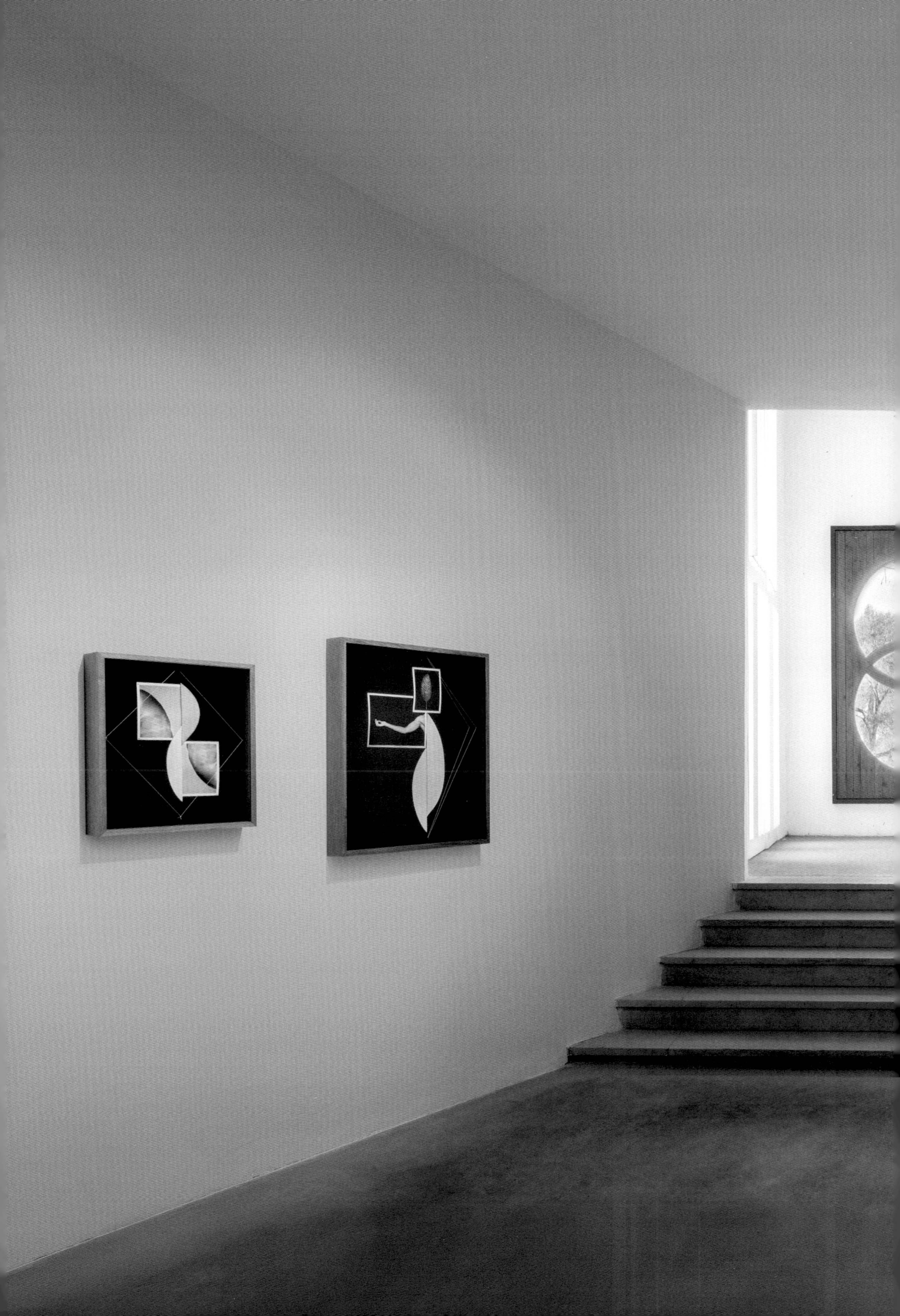

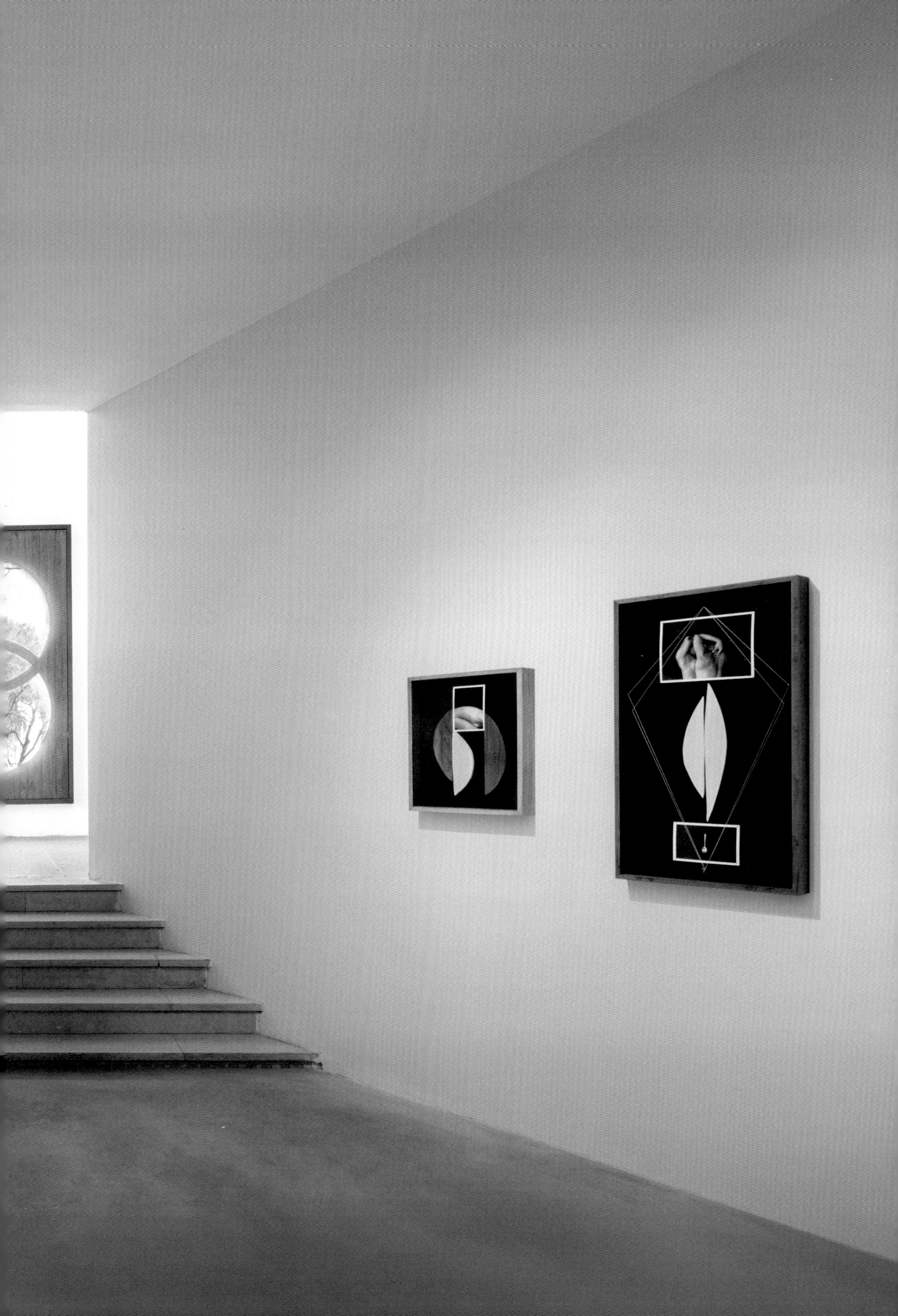

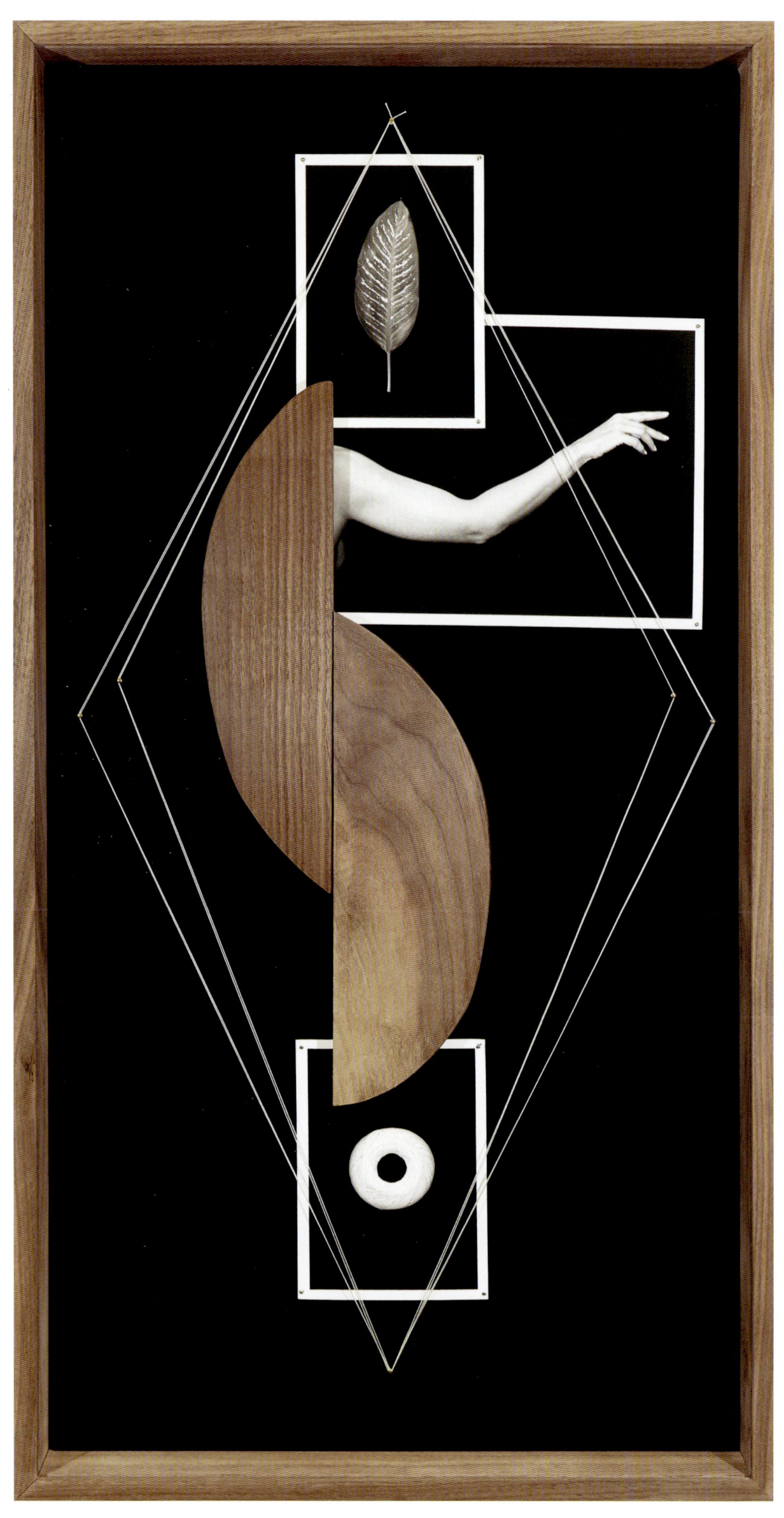

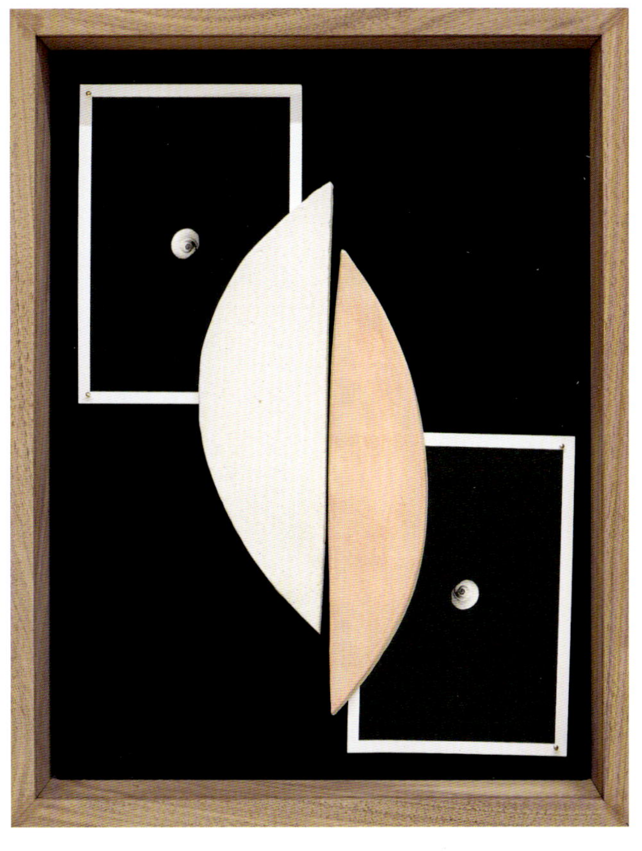

Feedback, 2020

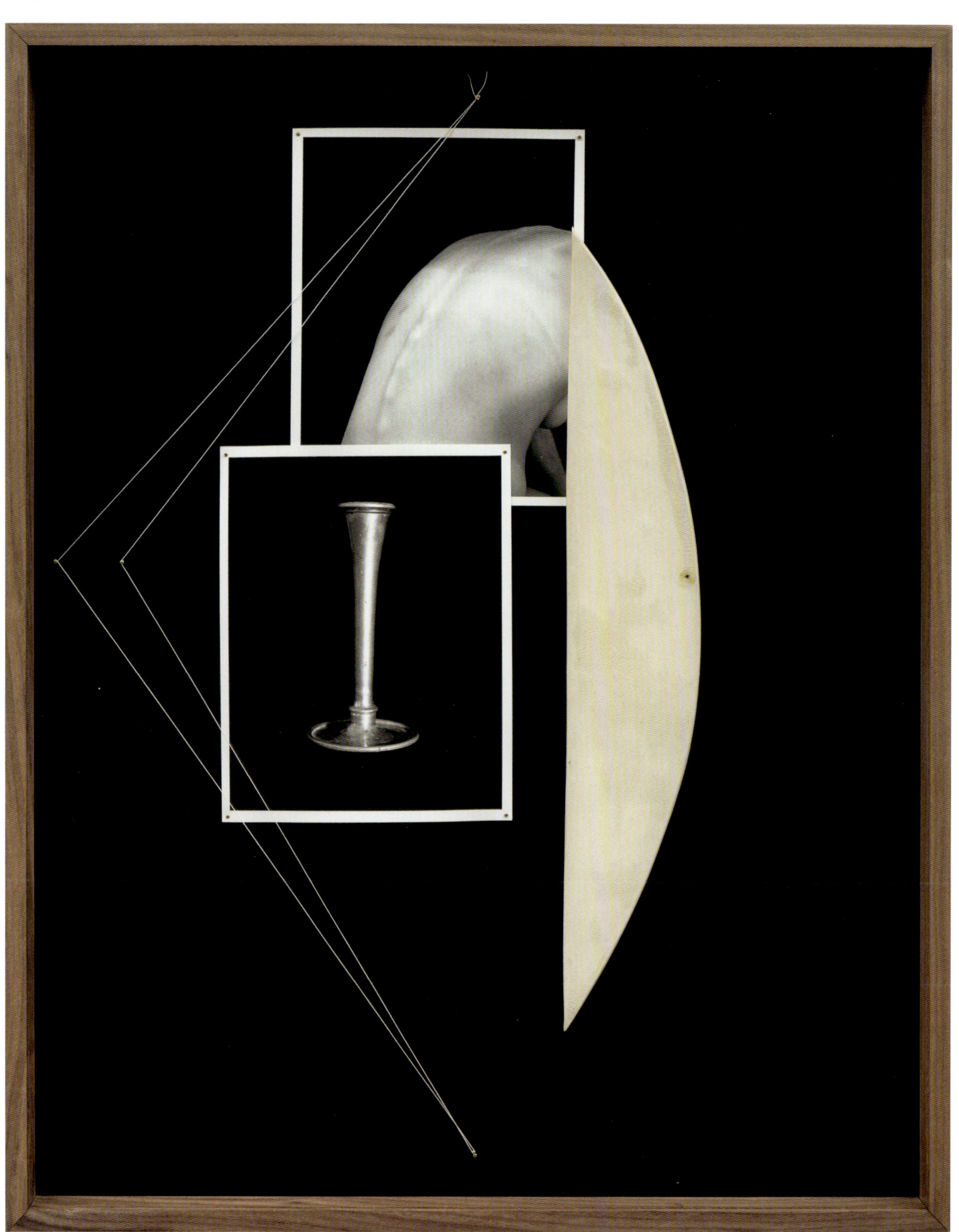

Cadence, 2022

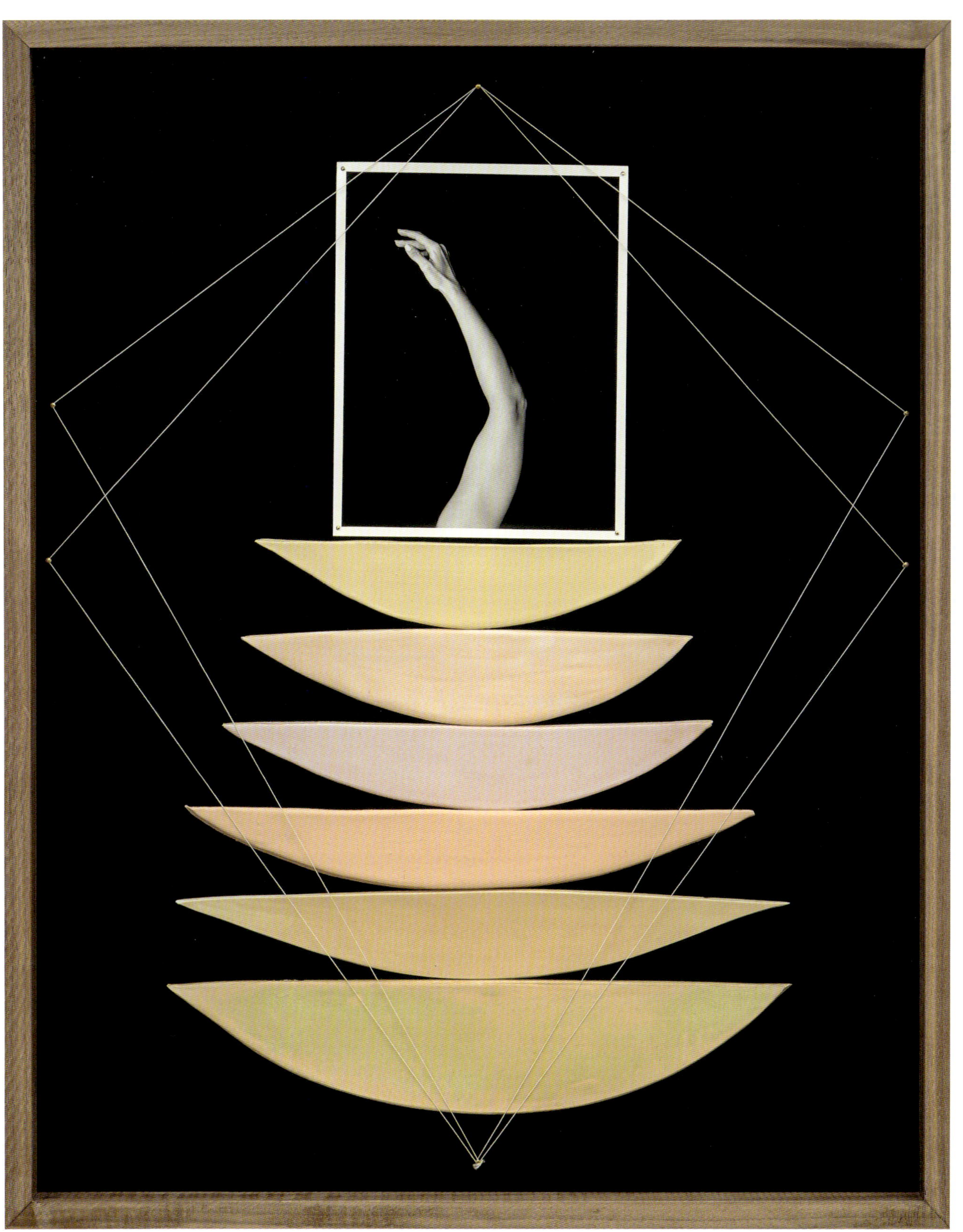

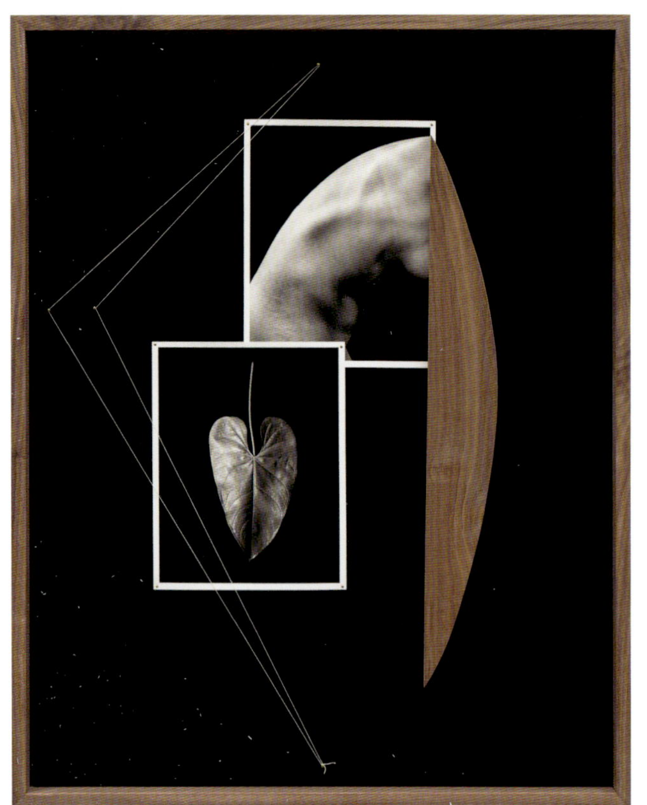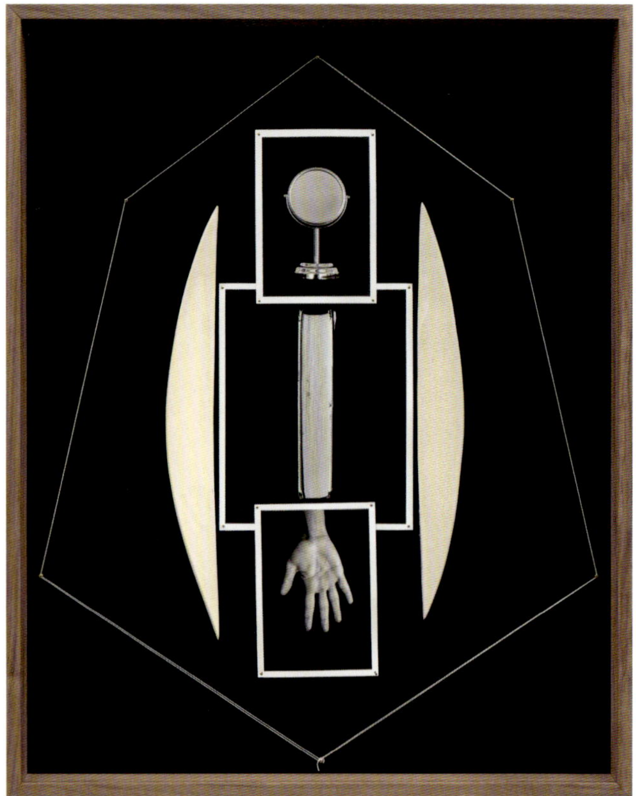

Circle Pose, 2023
Receiver, 2022

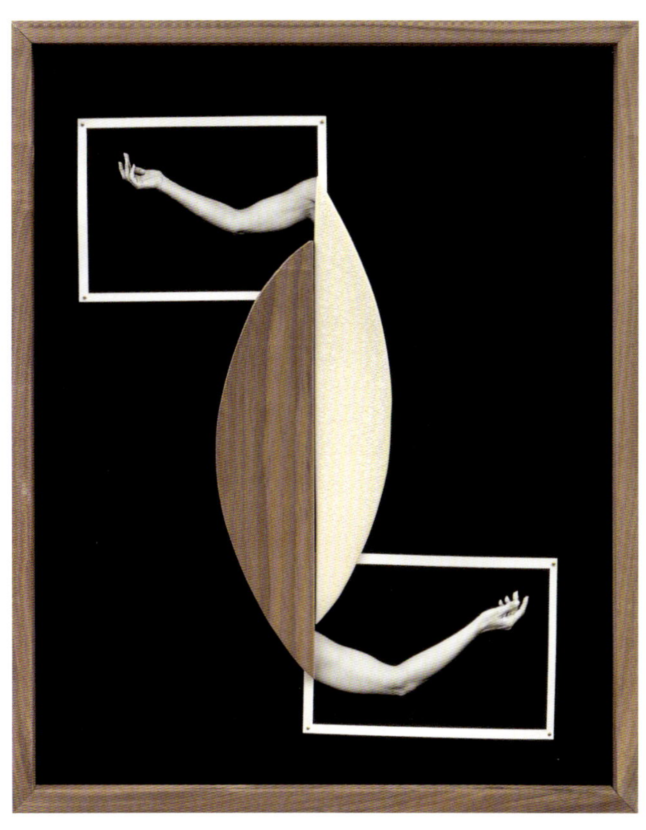

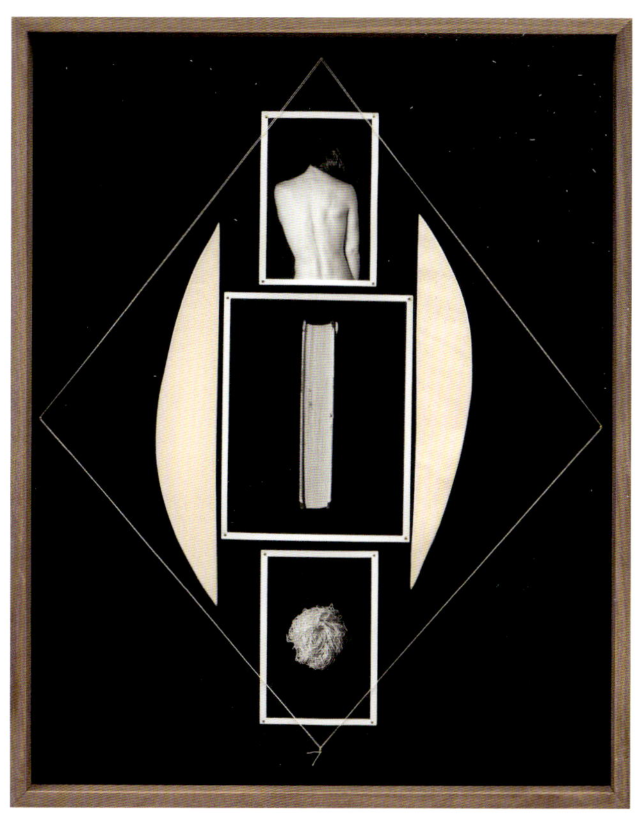

Radio, 2022
Author, 2022
→ The Milk of Dreams, 59th International Art Exhibition, Venice, 2022

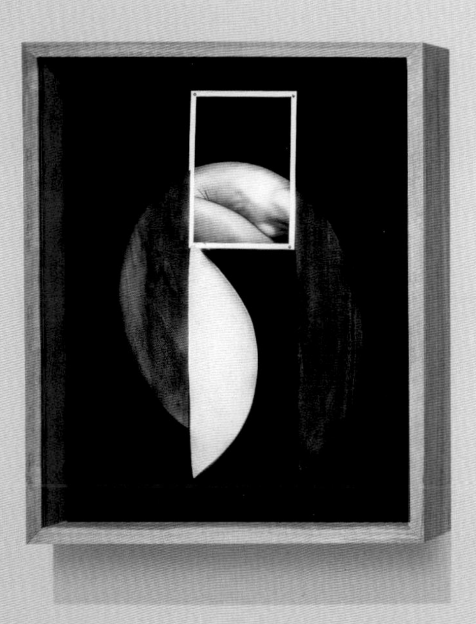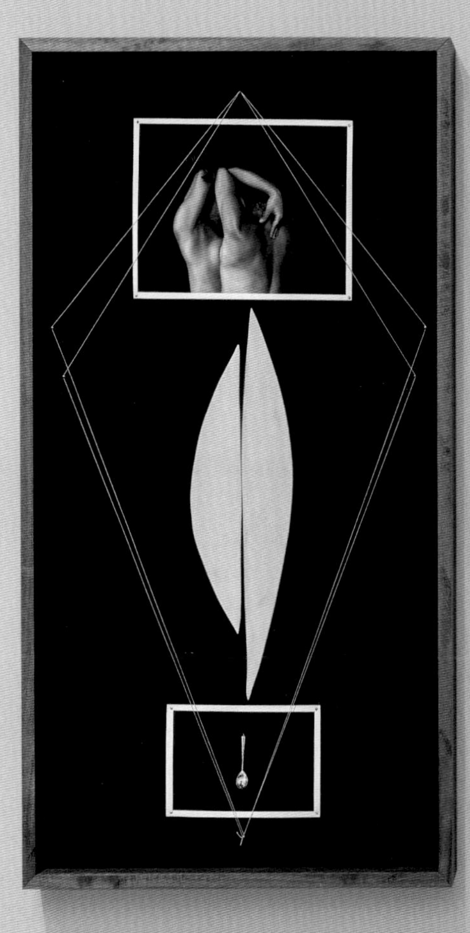

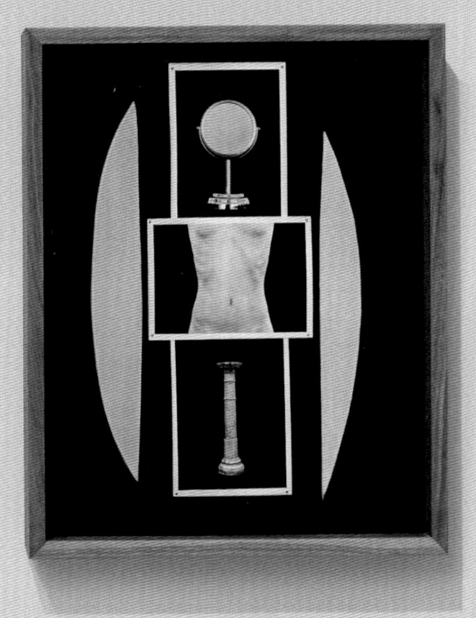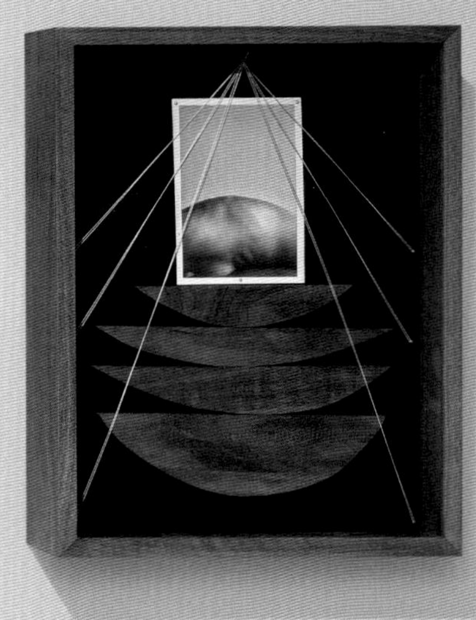

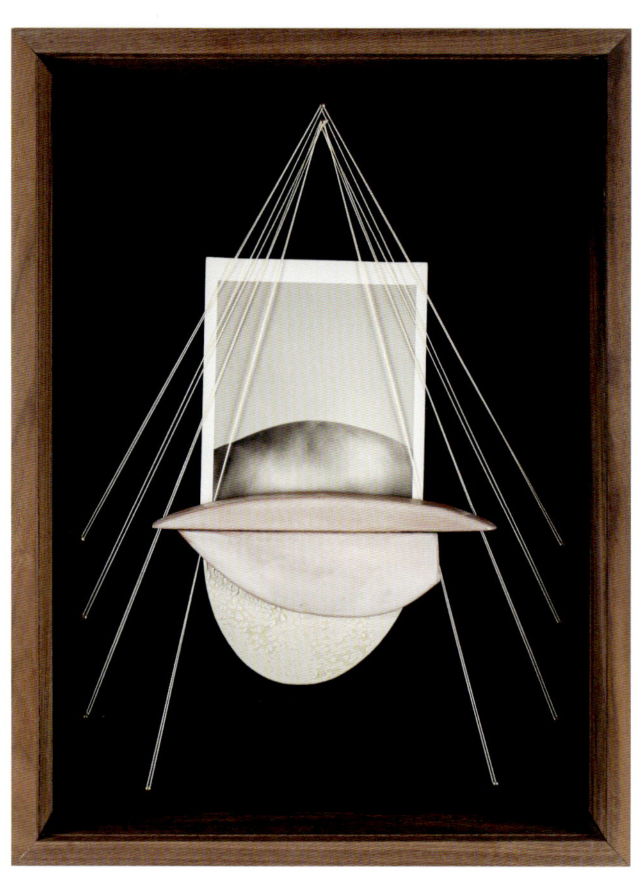

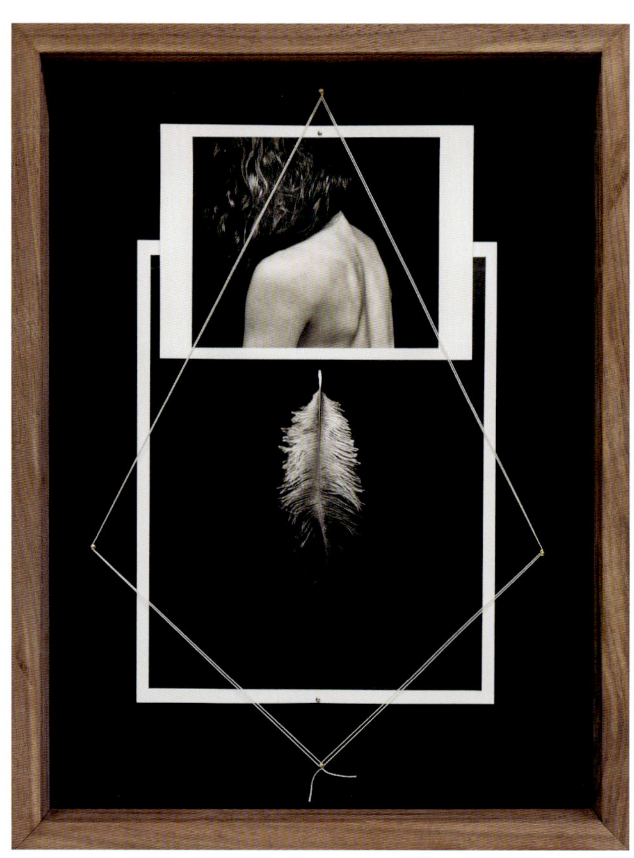

Empath, 2019
Musing, 2020

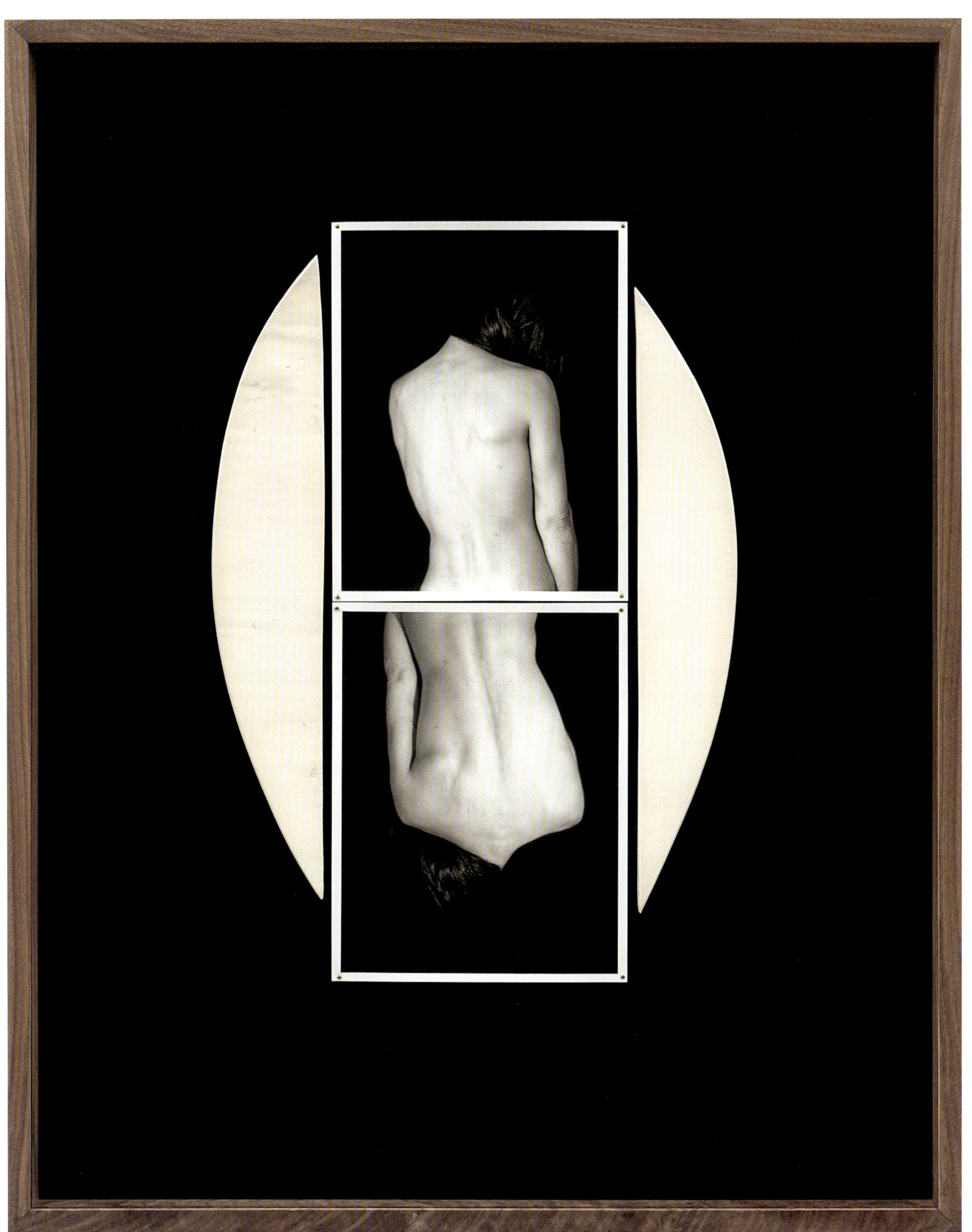

Parallel, 2022

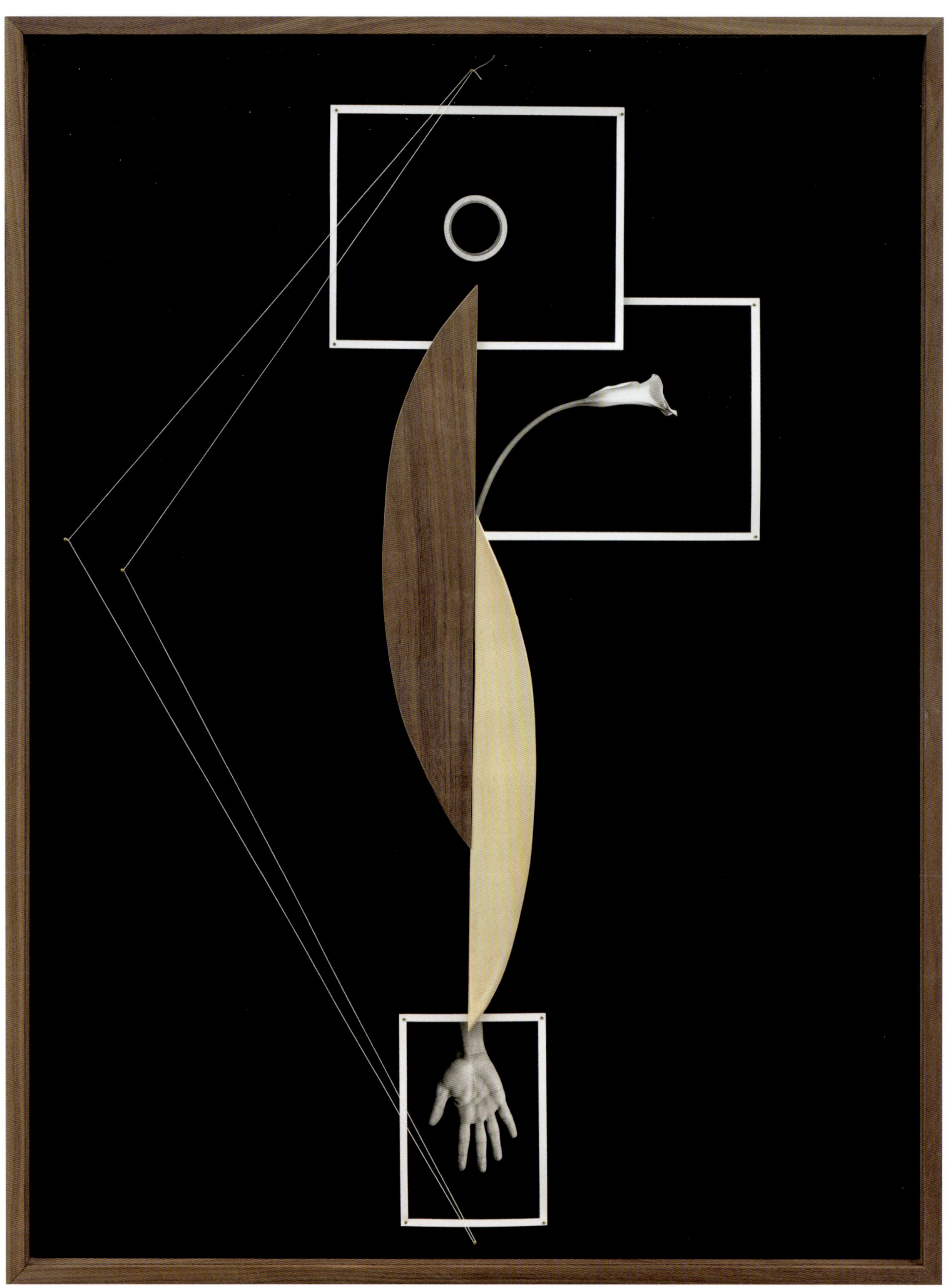

CC Sheree, it has been wonderful for me to see your preparation of this survey book that draws together a sampling of your practice over the past 13 years. Can I first ask you about your childhood, and when your relationship with art and art making began?

SH I was born in Isfahan, Iran, but grew up in North-West Ohio. My sister and I were very young when our parents moved from Iran to the United States to continue their post-grad education. As a result of the Islamic Revolution of 1979 in Iran, my family stayed in the US and my parents divorced. My mom was accepted to the medical College of Ohio in Toledo, where she was working toward her PhD in pharmacology, and where my sister and I moved. The US in the early 1980s was not a welcoming place for Iranians, and I grew up feeling socially and culturally ostracized. I loved to draw and when I was very young, and my mom sought out a drawing tutor for me to work with. Art was always something that I loved and felt like an arena where I could retreat, be thoughtful, and actively participate.

CC When did it fix in your mind that you would go to art school?

SH My mother was faculty at the University of Toledo, which meant I could go to school there for free; this was a determining factor of my undergrad studies, which I started at the University of Toledo in 1992. The art department was housed in the newly opened Center for the Visual Arts designed by Frank Gehry, and was located outside the main campus in downtown Toledo, connected to the Toledo Museum of Art. To be in an incredible art center and to also able to take classes outside of art—from creative writing and science to history and women's studies—was the right combination for me. Such a multi-disciplinary perspective also made me realize that art studio classes were my passion.

CC Tell me how your art practice began to take shape.

SH I was lucky that a new young professor fresh from New York, Deborah Orloff, had just started teaching at the University of Toledo Department of

Photography. Deborah exposed me to many living art-ists, including artists working with photography who she invited to give talks and do studio visits with us. In this time before social media or Internet research, I was so hungry to see and read everything I could find by working artists. I loved the work of Sophie Calle, Annette Messager, and Lorna Simpson. I was a very dedicated student and was able to study abroad at the Glasgow School of Art in Scotland for a term in 1998 and, in retrospect, I can see that the forging of my own practice was most clearly influenced by my experience there. I was in the Environmental Art program, which was focused on Conceptual and time-based art. I had a studio space and could concen-trate on my practice and garnering knowledge from wonderful speakers who came to the school, such as Chantal Akerman and Yinka Shonibare.

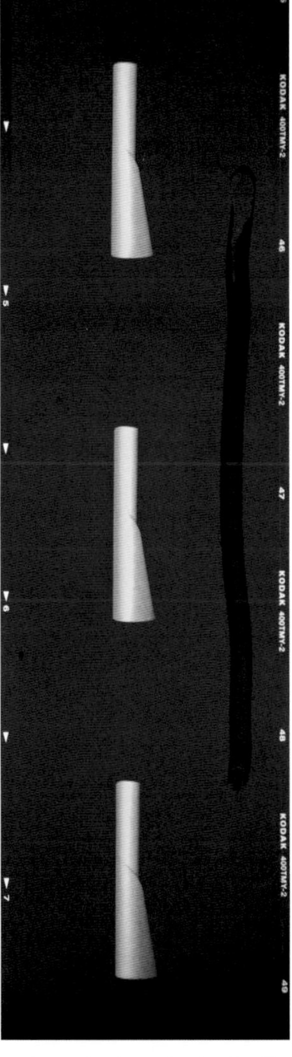

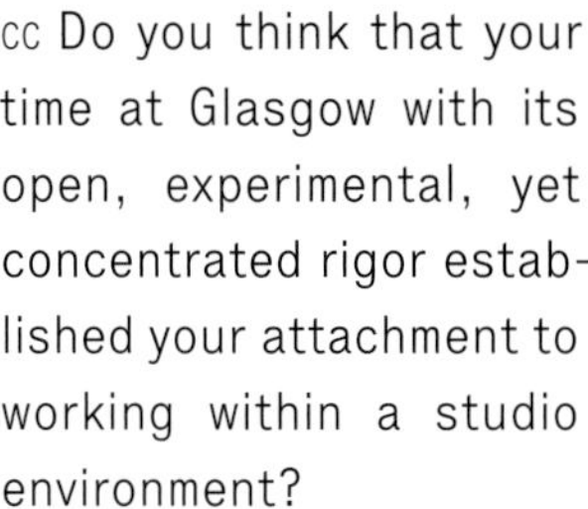

cc Do you think that your time at Glasgow with its open, experimental, yet concentrated rigor estab-lished your attachment to working within a studio environment?

sh It was the first time I had a designated studio space where I could figure things out. I remember taking local newspapers and using a heavy graphite pencil to blank out text, while leaving all of the words and phrases I didn't understand exposed. The papers covered the floor of my studio, exposing both my dili-gent work and my ignorance. I started making collages there, working with photographs and things I would collect, like train tickets and letters that came to me via postal mail.

cc I'm struck that all of the artists that you have cited as early shapers of your understanding of art were living artists.

sh By the time I went to Chicago to start my MFA in 2000, I had a sense of contemporary art as inhabited by living artists. I was also more generally conscious of how photography was slowly transforming from analog to digital at that time, and there was so much new technology that helped push the boundaries of what art could be. Studying photography as my major was my way into participating in the new art making, which was often time-based, performative, grappling with identity, constructed, and conceptual.

cc Why did you choose the School of the Art Institute in Chicago?

sh Deborah had brought Barbara DeGenevieve from the School of the Art Institute to the University of Toledo to give a lecture about her work and par-ticipate in our critique. Her talk completely blew me away and her critique shattered many of the ideas I had thought were true and important about my work. I knew I had to study with her. One of her favorite say-ings was "you can sleep when you're dead."

cc Tell me about the work you were making while at the Art Institute.

sh There was a lot of performative work using video, with an emphasis on the power dynamic between art-ist and model. My thesis project was a series called *The Artist/The Exhibitionist*. In my studio, I photo-graphed a man, an exhibitionist, while I recorded the entire session with video. There was an interesting power dynamic in the interplay of me needing to look at him for my graduation project, and him needing me to look at him for his pleasure. I was very interested in this exchange. I was trying my hardest to direct the situation and to see if it was possible for me to objec-tify him. The videos and stills I made are one thing, and the dialogue between us was another layer. Also in this series, I answered an ad for someone who was looking for a woman to photograph, and negotiated that I could take photographs while he was photographing me.

cc What you describe sounds pretty fearless, and I wasn't expecting you to say that.

sh I was so serious about my work, and I could disassociate from the situation and slip into a different persona. Under this guise, I felt strong and would do anything to push the work. I think this was a defense mechanism I had adapted from childhood, to mentally extract myself from an uncomfortable situation.

cc By this point, were you decided about sustaining a studio-based practice and being part of the contemporary art world?

sh It was very unclear to me what I should be doing, and I stayed in Chicago after I graduated. My boyfriend at the time, later husband, Rashid [Johnson] was coming up through the same program that I had just graduated from at the Art Institute, and he was actively showing his work internationally even before graduation. He exposed me to a lot within the worlds of art and the gallery structure, and he was very clear about wanting to move to New York. I had always wanted to live in New York, but I held back until 2006, working and saving money. Also, my sister was moving to Chicago and I wanted to help her get settled.

cc Your sister is your long-term model, and her gestures and physicality are depicted in your work. When did you start working together?

sh She has modeled for me since I was an art student. We are physically similar and in the context of my practice and my work, I think of her as a stand-in for my own body. When we are in my studio working, there is no boundary between us. When she sits for me, our closeness makes me feel like I am almost in possession of her body.

cc Did you establish your studio practice soon after you came to New York in the mid-2000s?

sh It wasn't immediate, and I was sharing studios for years, working in small spaces while I had jobs in bars to make money. I was making still life and small sculptures to photograph, created with ephemeral objects like balloons and things that you might get at a party store.

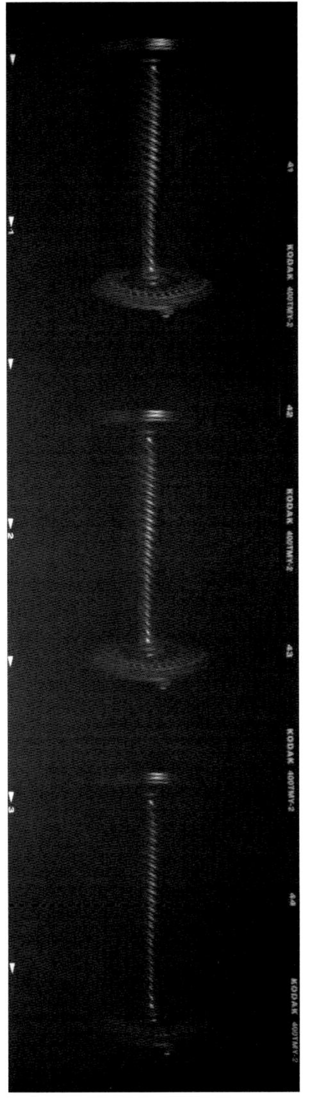

cc In the 2000s, were you already working with black and white film photography?

sh No, I was shooting color transparencies, working with Ektachrome.

cc What do you think attracted you to Ektachrome at that time?

sh I think it was partly an economic decision. It wasn't the most expensive, and you could see what you had when you shot it. I think I had somehow got it into my head that color transparency film was a more professional type of photography.

cc I imagine it was still within that expansive, sweet spot in the mid-to-late 2000s when digital backs on professional SLR cameras were becoming the professional default, but you could still find this jewel-like, exacting transparency film. It hadn't disappeared. For me, your use of analog film, and the discipline of lighting still life in your studio immediately connects you with a wonderful constellation of artists [Liz Deschenes, Eileen Quinlan, Erin Shirreff, Sara VanDerBeek] who were coming out of MFA programs at the same time, who were very conscious of their active choices in "making" images in an increasingly dematerialized digital image world, and animating the heightened sense of photography's "objecthood."

sh I think that's probably a world of artists that I was hoping to be part of rather than what I felt I was within. I was deep into the solitary process of finding things on the street, bringing them into my studio, and working out how to incorporate them into these temporary sculptures, and how to activate them in my photographs. I also still loved the romantic process of making photographs. It was very much a time of growth for me, of just moving the practice along, pulling things

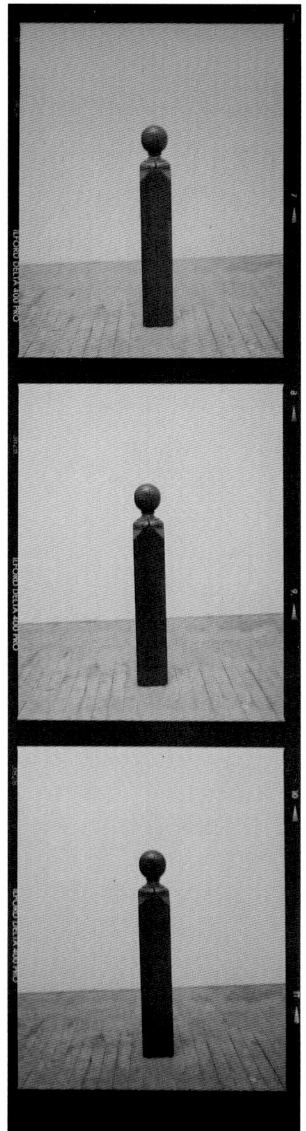

together, and locating them in my studio in ways that felt true to me. Aside from residencies, I wasn't showing the work until the 2010s.

CC It seems to me, in a photographic sense, that you were establishing the methodologies that we can see in this monograph in work made from 2012 onward. I wonder if those early years in New York were also when you established your full range of material vocabulary and the ways in which the non-photographic, or perhaps materials and processes, intersect with photographic prints.

SH To a certain extent, yes. For instance, I have used string and thread in my studio for a while. I taught myself macramé and used those pieces in later collages. I would find cast-off pieces of wood outside my studio that I would carve and photograph or use as elements in collages. I was as continually busy with my hands as I am now. It was also a time to educate myself in the New York-specific artworld and to think about the relationship that photography has to abstraction as well as to painting, which was the most dominant medium.

CC Once you step outside of the automated defaults of photography and you work against or beyond that, it brings you into a world of materiality, and one with a gestural physicality that can be equal parts painterly, sculptural, as well as photographic.

SH I think it has also been about the performative for me. One of the earliest works in this book is from the *Sleight of Hand* series (2013) where I was in a studio environment, thinking about how I could activate a space and record my presence. I used a film camera, making multiple exposures of the process of removing sheets of paper taped to the wall, intentionally recording in one photographic frame the duration of a series of minimal gestures. I saw this as an expansion of the decisive moment in photography, as well as an additive process which I equated with drawing or painting.

CC The *Sleight of Hand* series also has one of the hallmarks of your photographic work in that the studio floor and wall are present as both subject and contextual frame. For me it's also a strategy that signals or time stamps the performative process within your studio.

SH The studio becomes the stage that holds the work. I was also thinking a lot about the horizon lines in Mark Rothko's paintings and using the studio wall and floor as a way of marking that bisection. On many levels, I was learning and experimenting with abstract gestures.

CC And that includes your darkroom work of that time, making these animated and distinctly large photograms.

SH With the photograms, the sleight of hand of my practice happened in the darkroom. I would take in paper and a blade and my cell phone as a light source. I think of the process as very much like drawing—of me finding marks that I liked and trying to make abstract compositions with them.

CC There's also a very deliberate textural quality to them: the way that you allow the wet analog darkroom processes to drip and slide over the paper.

SH It's textural, and physical, and it's figurative. My body is directly involved in the making—rolling out the paper, cutting out forms, as a shield from the light in a darkroom. The large photograms in my series called *Domes* (2014, slang for "heads") are figurative.

CC This figuration is amplified in your exhibition installations and the ways in which you arrange the photograms with your quite vertical, line-like bronze sculptures. I think they carry equivalent textural, physical, and figurative qualities. As a process, it seems like their character is held in the ephemeral state of the wax from which the casting mold for bronze is made—its own negative-to-positive process.

SH Yes, with the wax melting away and the bronze filling the space. The bronzes move between abstraction and figuration. I was looking at ancient Roman and Greek sculpture and intentionally mimicking contrapposto. I wanted to allude to a history of figuration and mark making that was far longer than photography. I think of this way of working as the same sensibility as in my drawings—an intuitive and additive process, something that you build up over time.

CC Your drawings are large pieces where you shift the direction of printing pigment by tilting the paper.

SH I was really attracted to the deep blackness of the photographic ink that you put in an inkjet printer. I was using large rolls of drawing paper that were similar to the large rolls of photographic paper I used in the darkroom. I use a syringe to apply the ink onto the paper laid on the floor and begin tilting the paper to direct the ink. I was moving and using my physical body in tandem with leaving much to chance and the will of the materials, in the same way that I was doing in the darkroom with my large photograms. I call the drawings a "mediated" way of mark making—not direct. To me, it is another manifestation of recording performance within a certain time and space.

CC All within the artist's studio that holds performance, placement, arranging together, recording, and fixing. All of those qualities and stages are also manifest in your framed assemblages. Can you tell me what the assemblages mean to you?

SH In general, I like the freedom of assemblages to bring together a balance of the photographs with the other ways that I use my hands such as the macramé threading, whittling wood, making shapes and impressions with ceramic clay, gathering found objects that I introduce into my studio. Again, I think what I am doing is a balance between abstraction and figuration.

CC I realize that, from a viewer's vantage point, I can't work out whether your assemblages are quick to make or take a long time. I know that each process demands hours of working with a material in your studio to understand its "will" as you call it, but I don't know how that translates into a complete assemblage work.

SH An assemblage is made through the act of play and experimentation in the studio with the materials I make separately. I have piles of the constituent parts—my vocabulary—and then it's a game to find their placement. There's the threat of failure in both the

making of the parts from ceramics to whittled wood where minute details give them their character, and the threat of failure in assembling and balancing them together into a piece. With the more recent assemblage works where I used ceramics, string, and photographs, I'm most conscious that I'm assembling a body—an exquisite corpse built from the vocabulary of images. In earlier work where I used wood, I was thinking more about the figure with a ground, within a landscape.

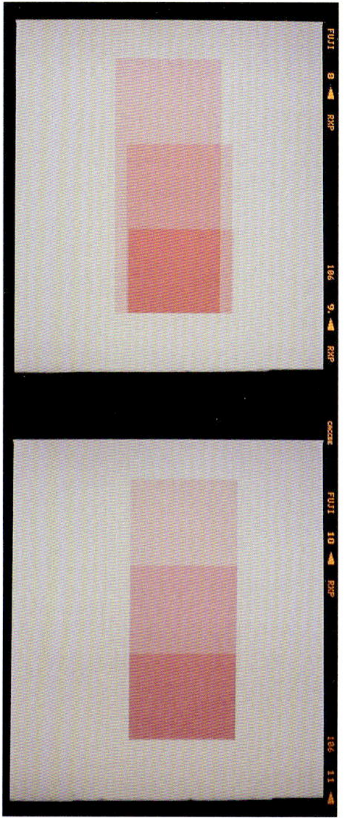
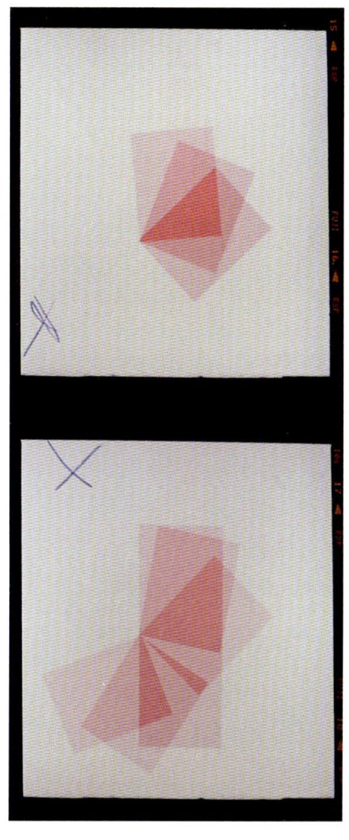

CC All the time that I'm listening to you, I'm thinking about how your practice is truly contingent on the physical and intellectual space of the studio. I'm also thinking about how that stays with the work once it's public, experienced in your exhibition installations. The title of one of the earliest works in this book (*Sleight of Hand*) is at the forefront of my thoughts about the effect of your work as a viewer, and the visual puzzling you provide us. You bring us into very close proximity to your studio practice: the contingent balance between elements in an assemblage work and the contingencies between works in a gallery installation. Would you describe exhibition making as an additional or the final step in your practice?

SH Maybe exhibition making is like a thread in my practice. I am interested in creating a narrative between the materials and the objects I choose to photograph. Many of the components of the collage allow me to work with my hands which is a very satisfying practice for me and allows me to put in the hours to physically understand its material language. I feel that I'm still learning. In my recent exhibitions, I have been intent on creating a direct parallel between my studio, and the experience of an exhibition of my work, and thinking about how the viewer's body relates to that space and the physicality of my practice. It's a further abstraction of my studio, but one where there is a sense of me standing alongside you as you encounter the work.

Artists mentioned in this conversation: Chantal Akerman (1950–2015); Sophie Calle (b. 1953); Barbara DeGenevieve (b. 1947); Annette Messager (b. 1943); Deborah Orloff (b. 1964); Mark Rothko (1903–1970); Yinka Shonibare (b. 1962); Lorna Simpson (b. 1960)

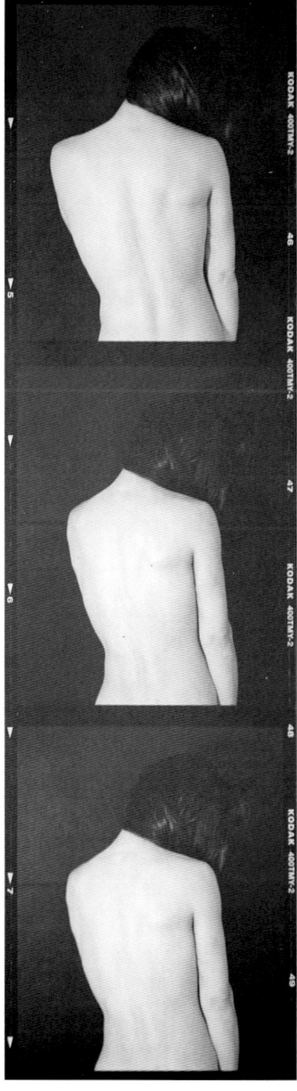
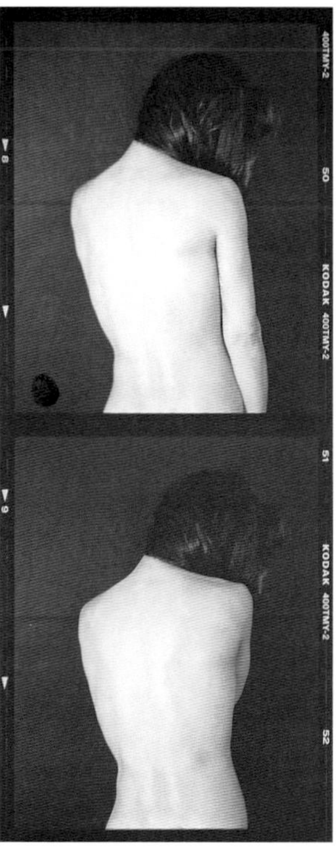

[p. 22–26] Contact sheets, 2012–2022
→ *As It Is*, 2017

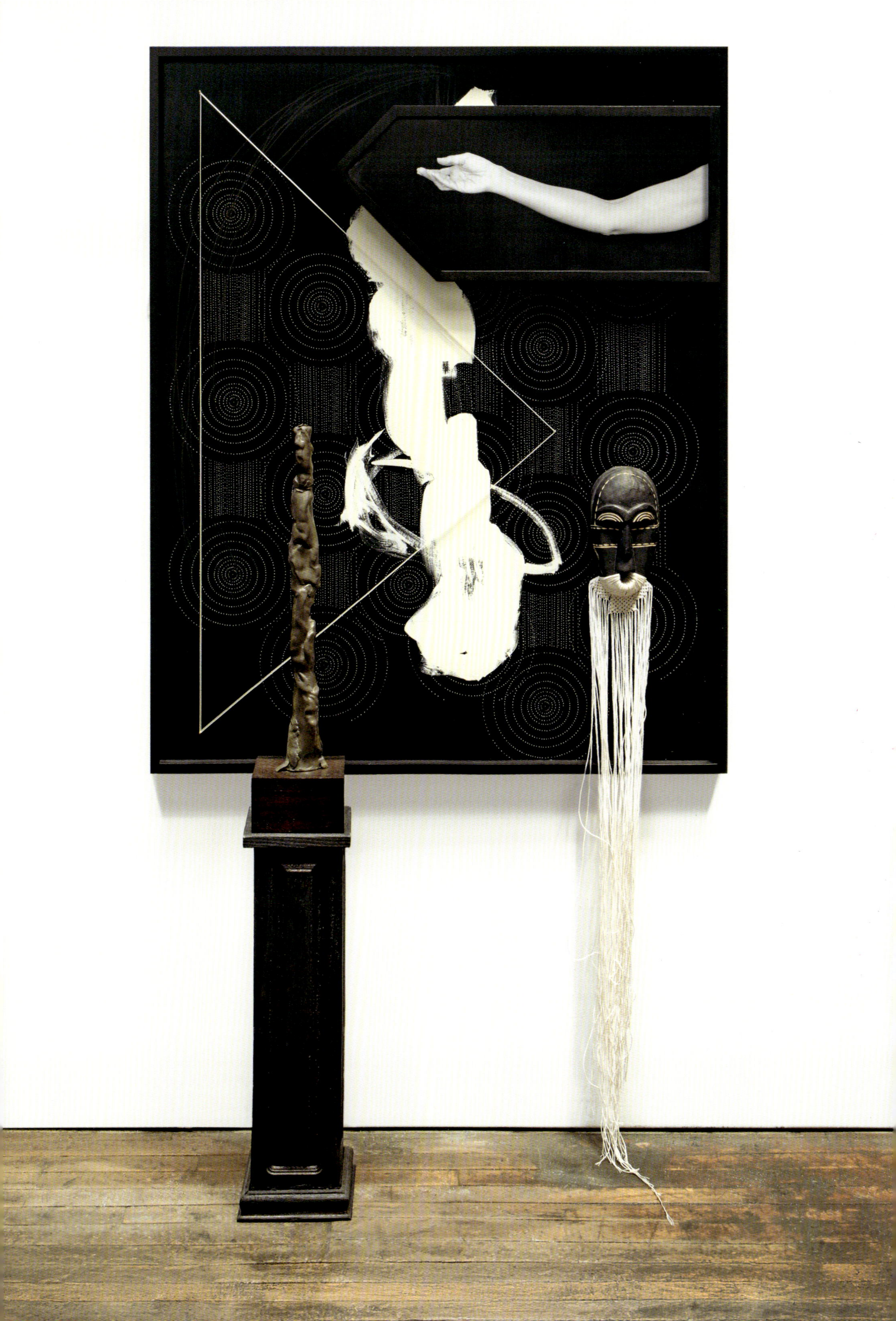

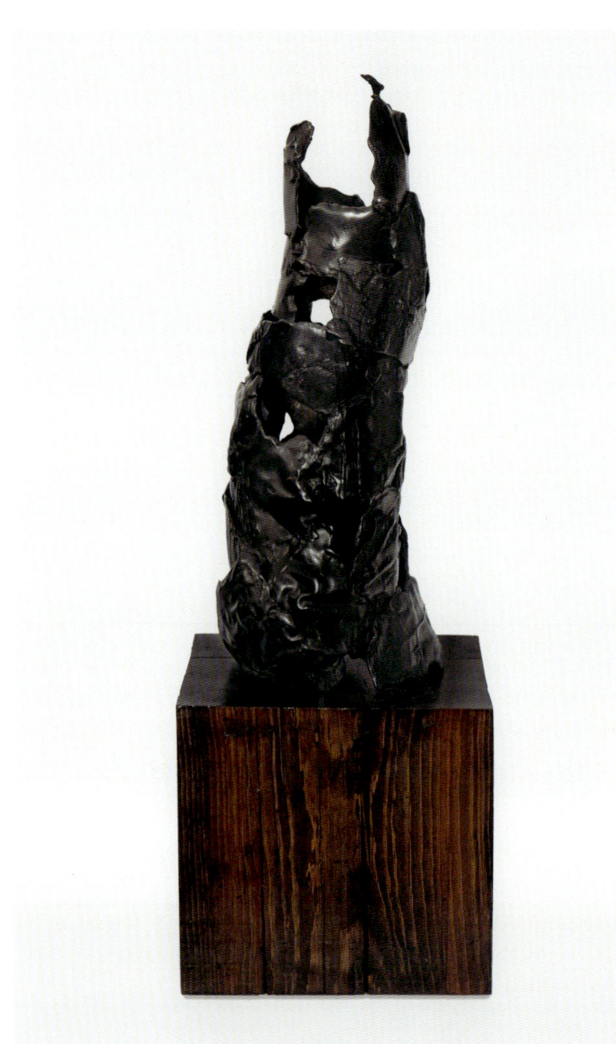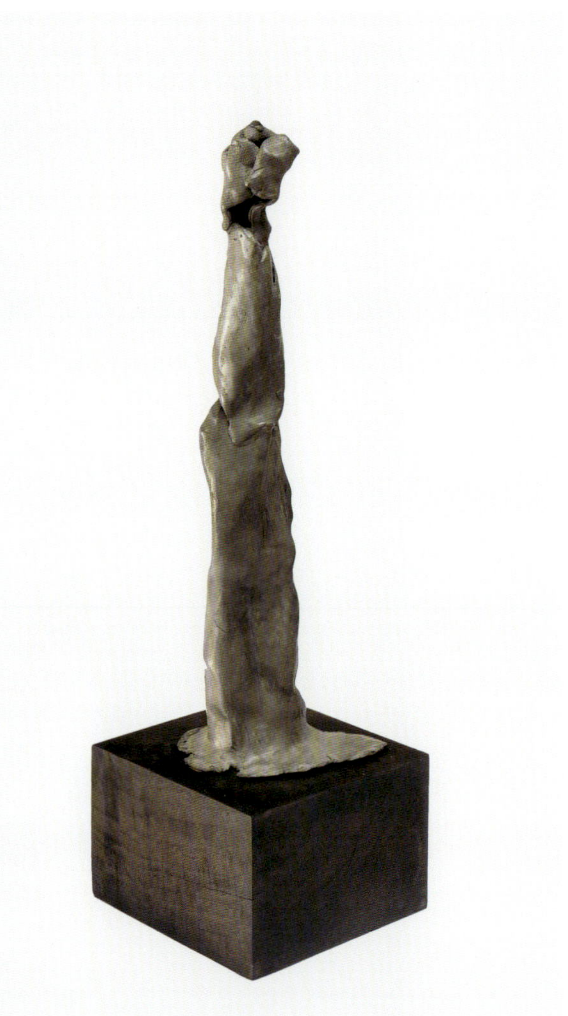

Kore, 2014
Proxy, 2014
→ *Domes*, Bischoff/Weiss Gallery, London, 2013

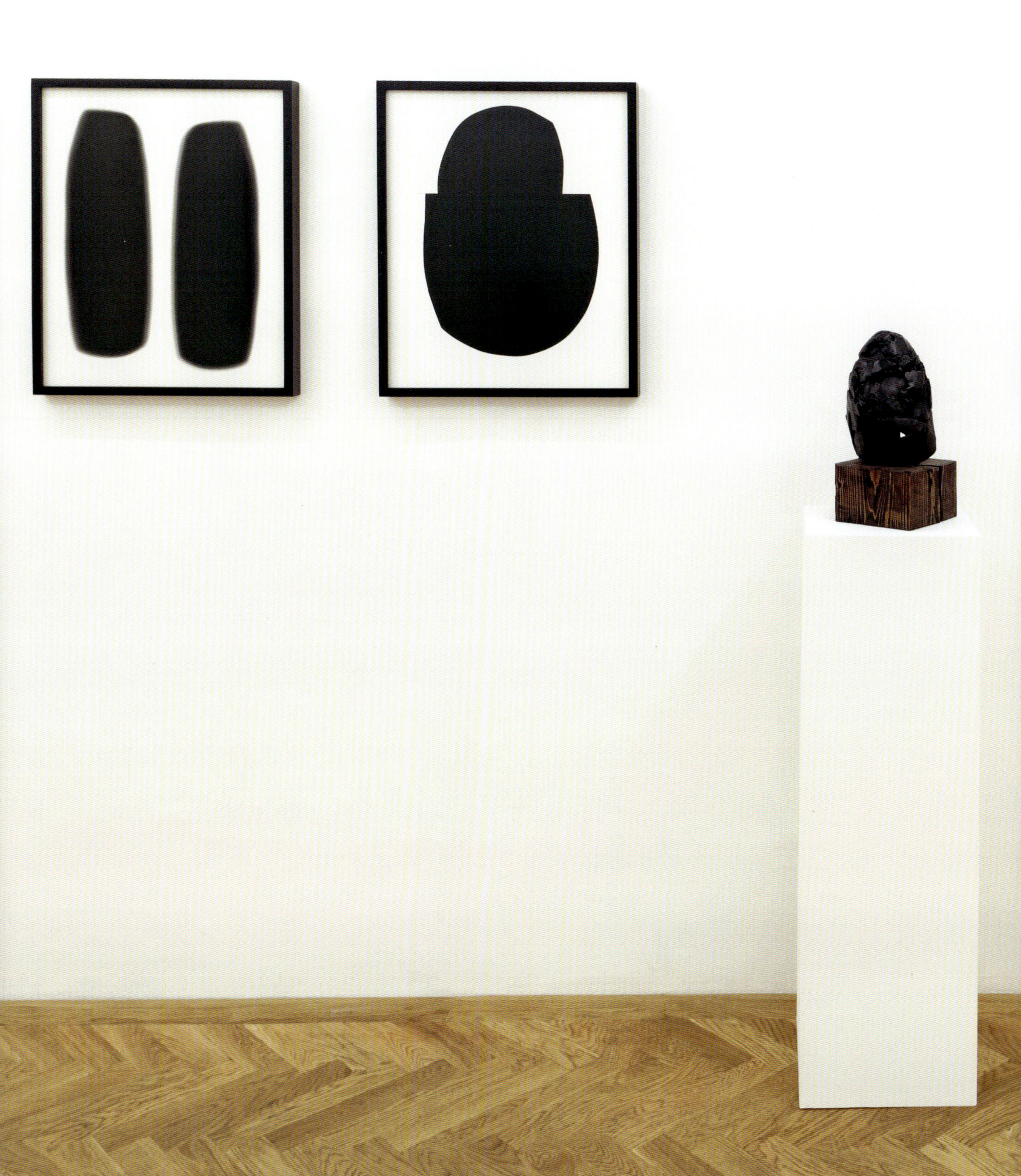

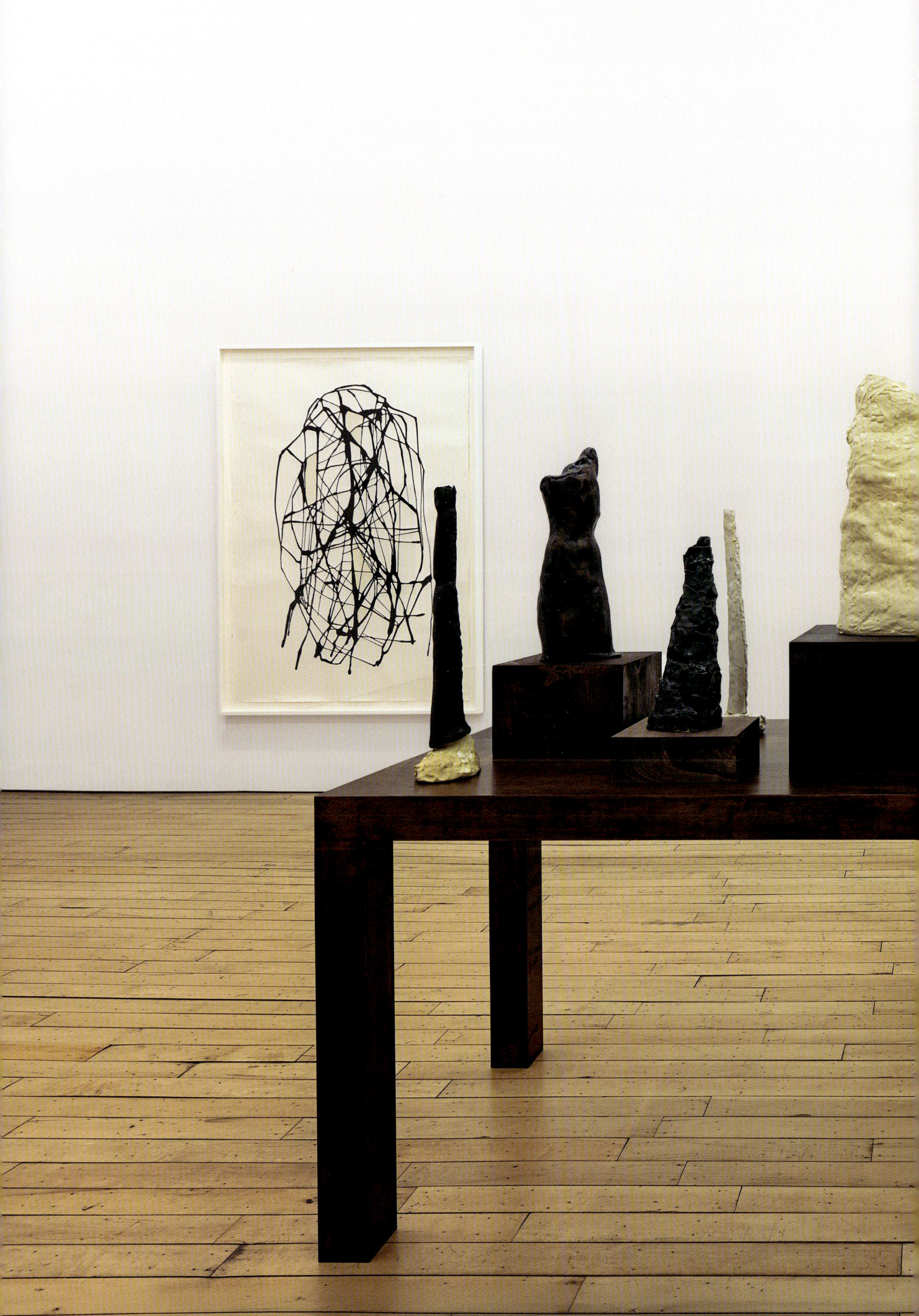

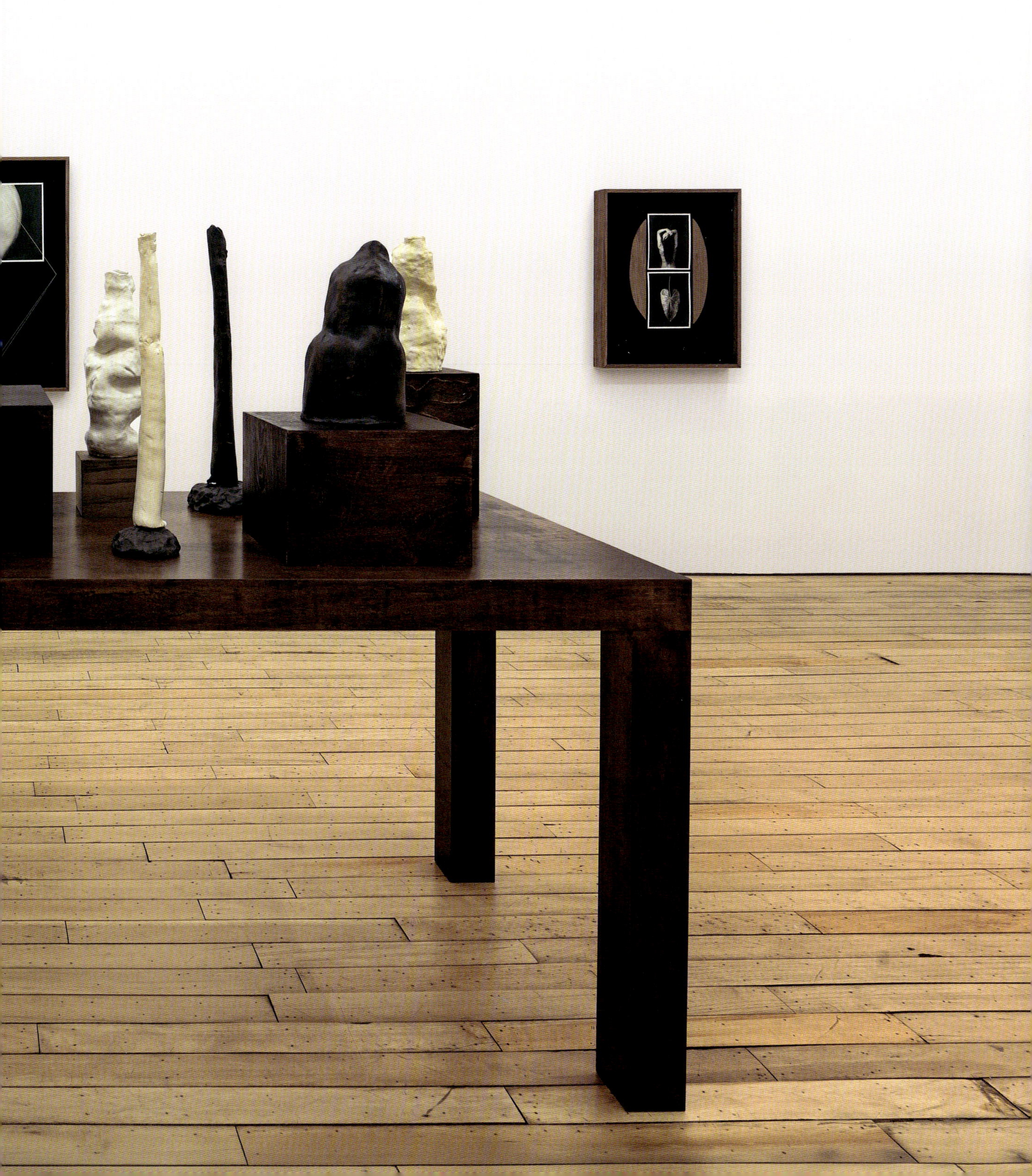

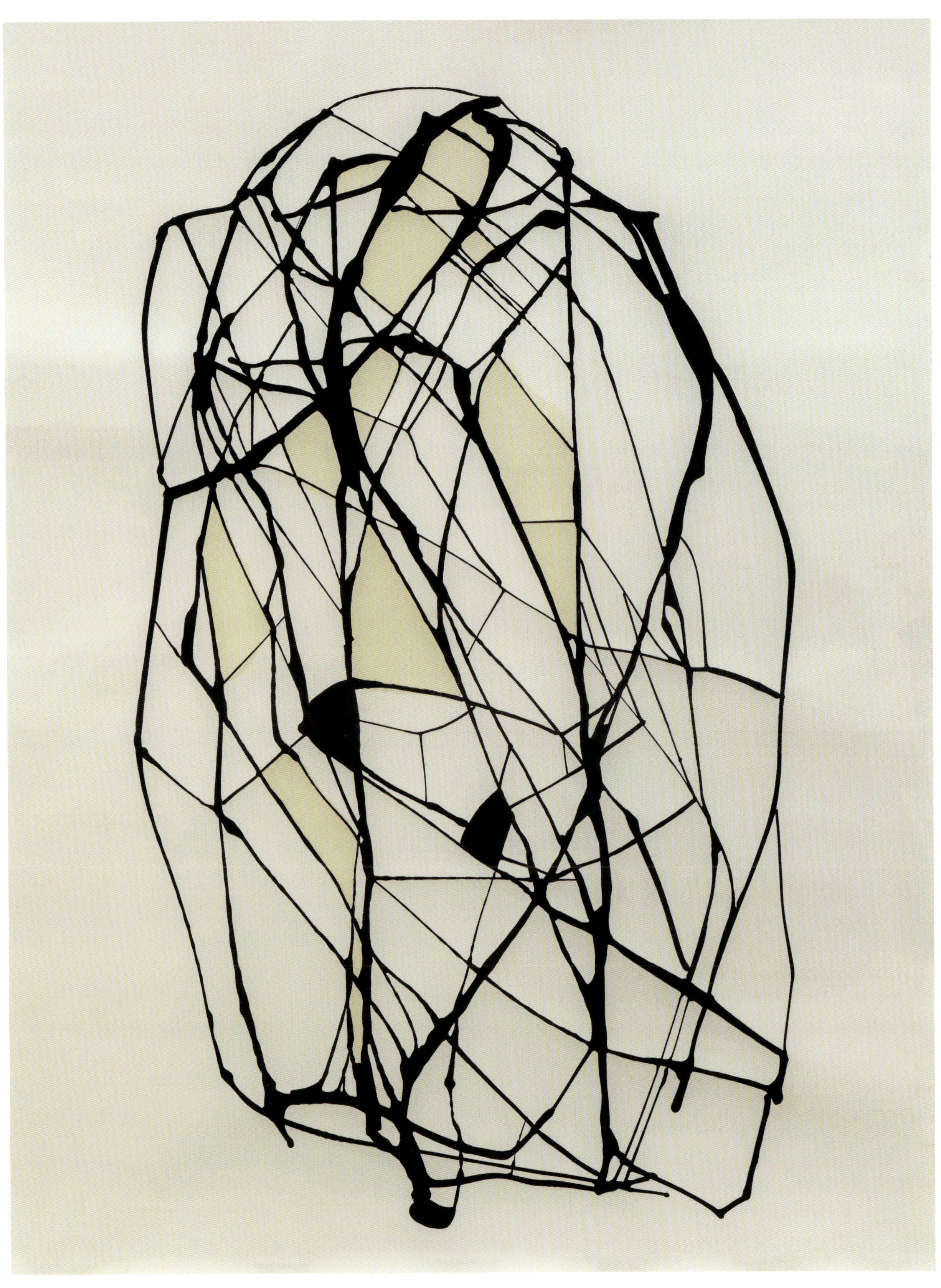

Untitled #2, Muscle Memory series, 2022
← *Leaning In*, Rachel Uffner Gallery, New York, 2022

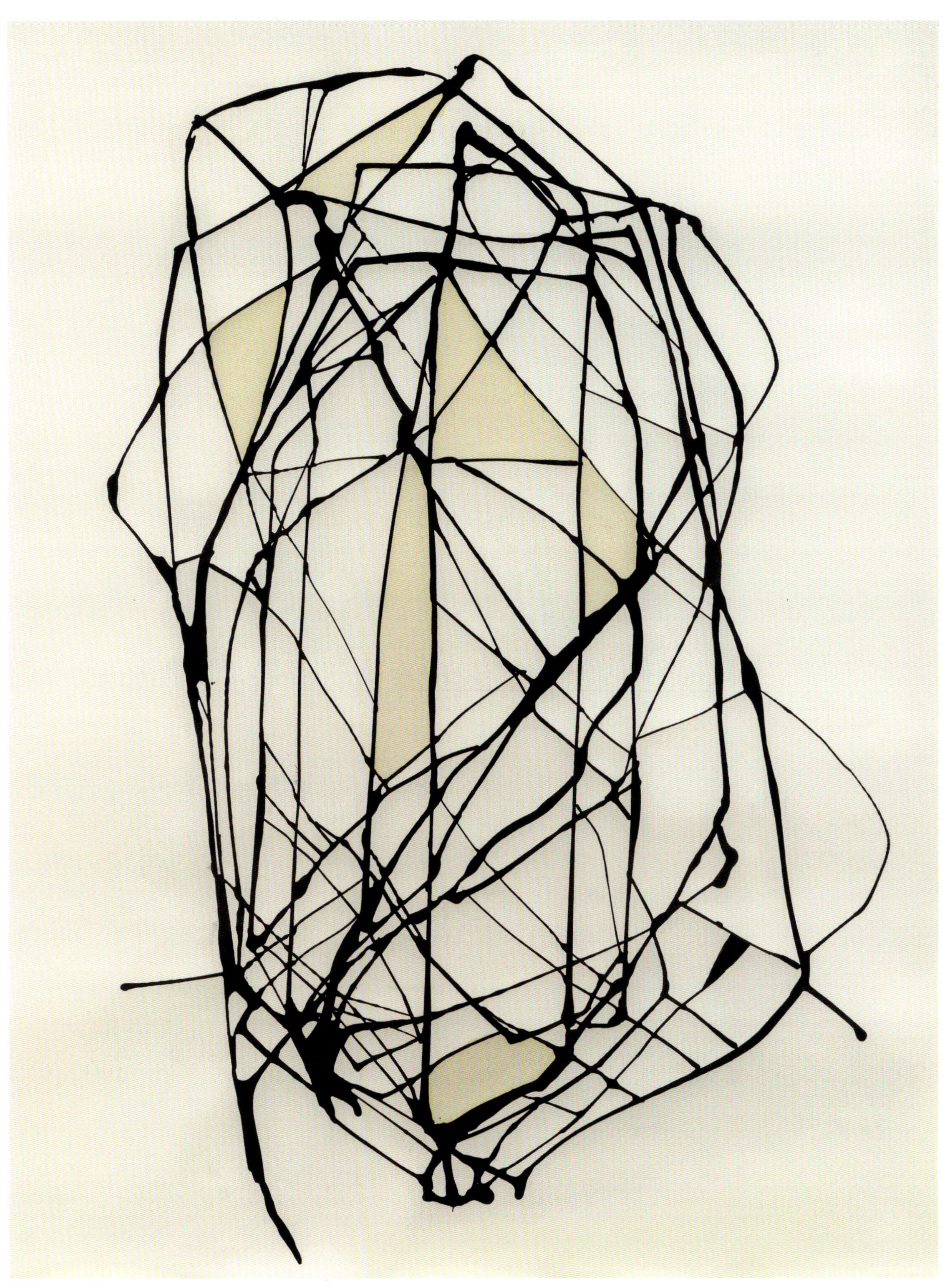

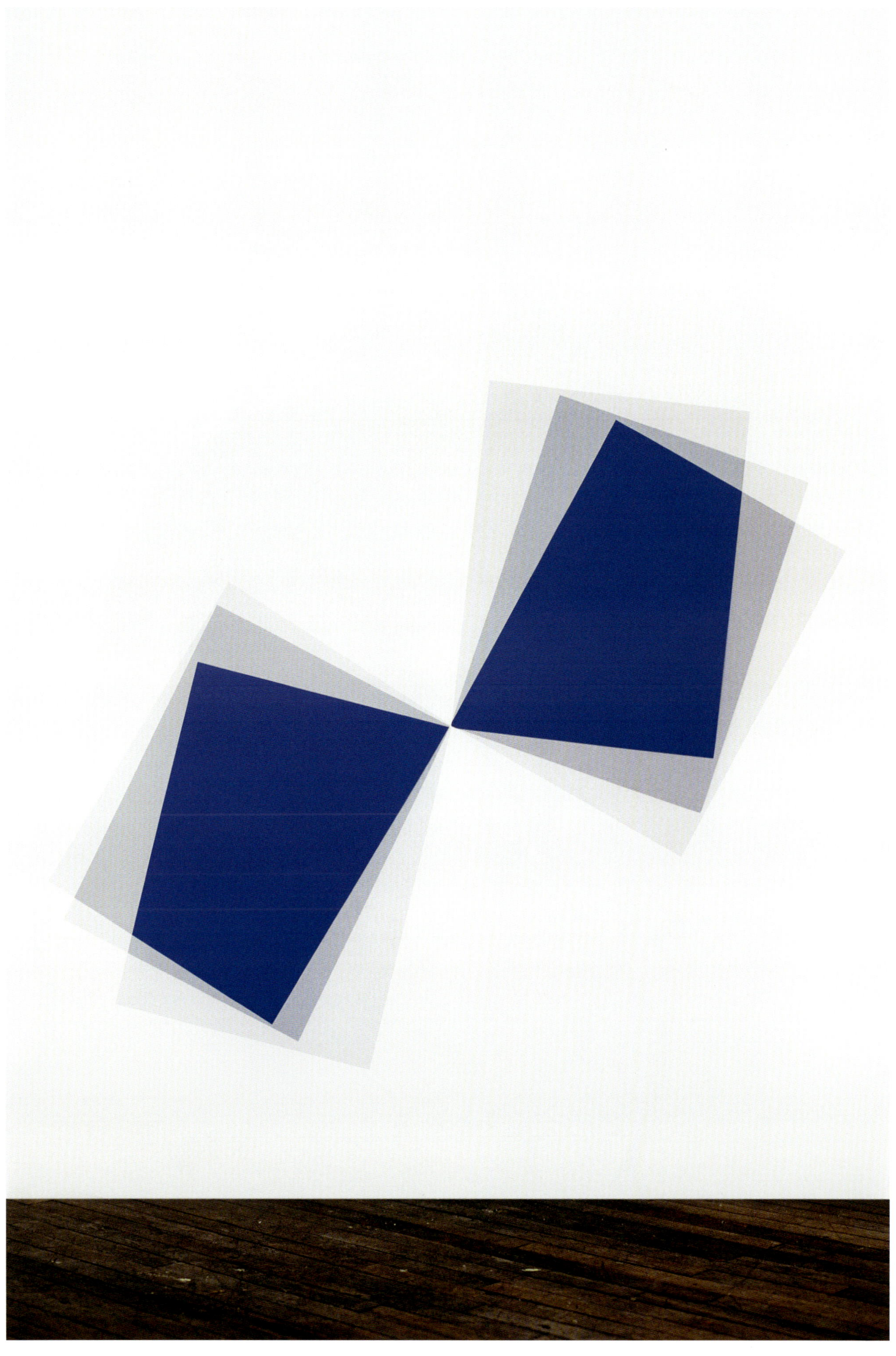

Sleight of Hand #78, 2013

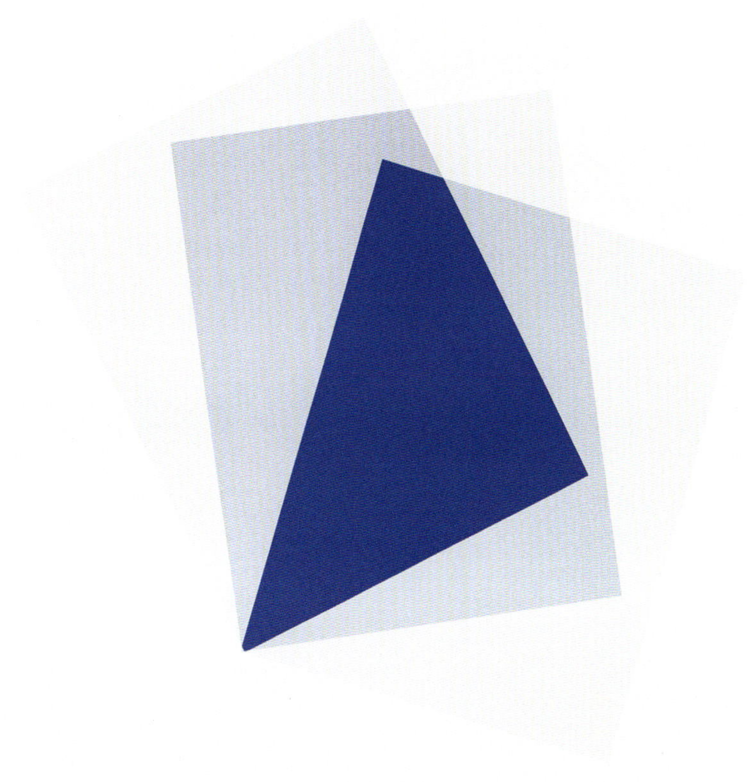

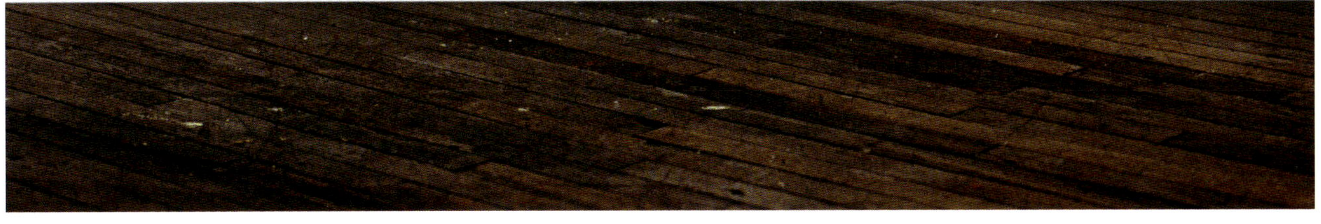

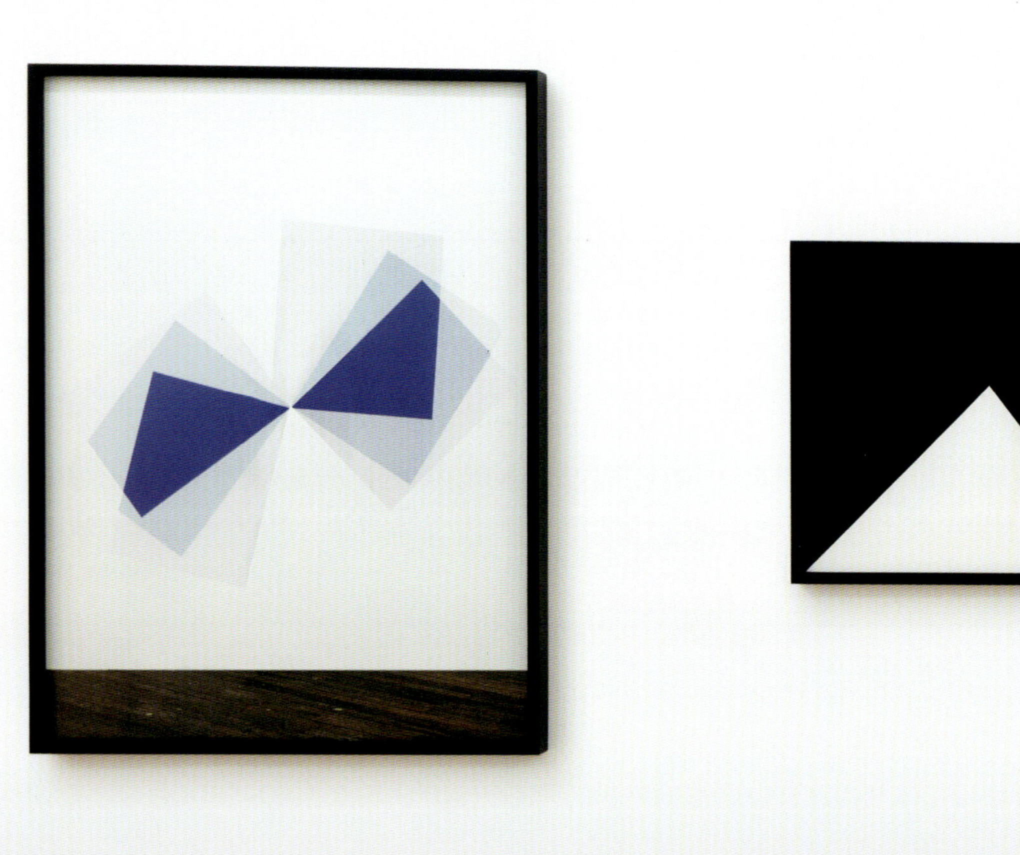
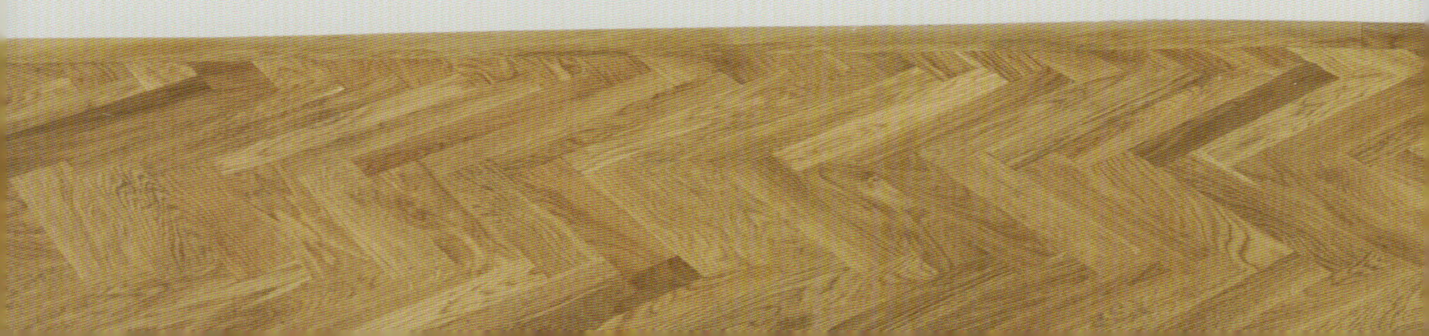

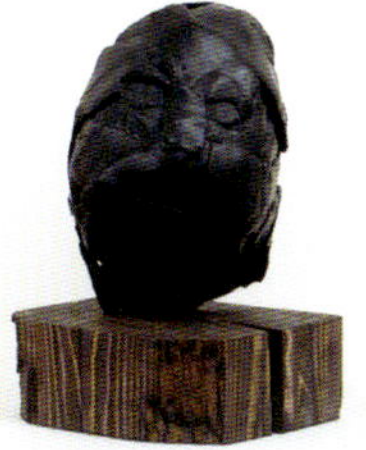

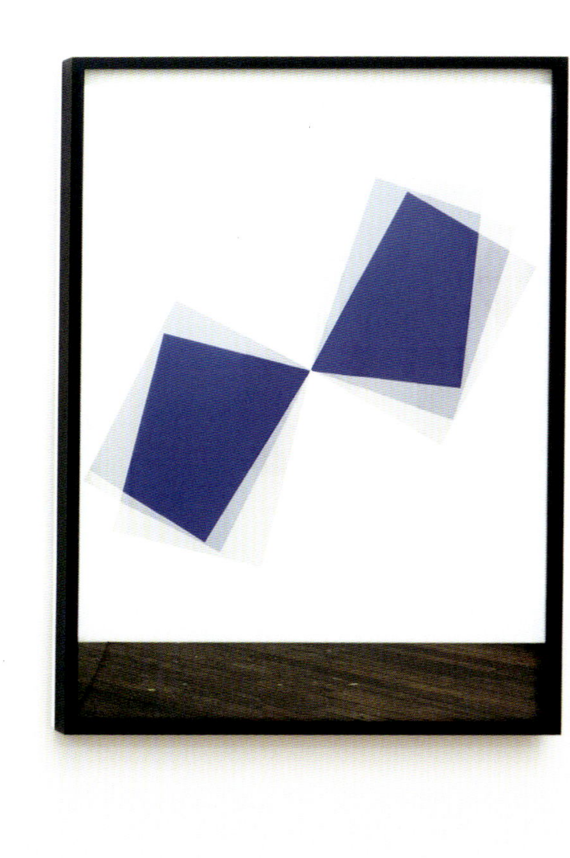

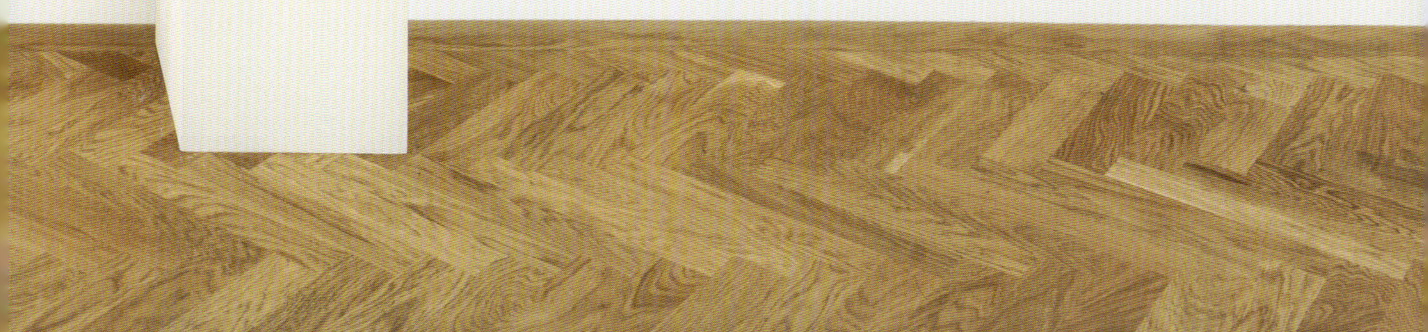

Sleight of Hand #4, 2013
Sleight of Hand #5, 2013
← *Domes*, Bischoff/Weiss Gallery, London, 2013

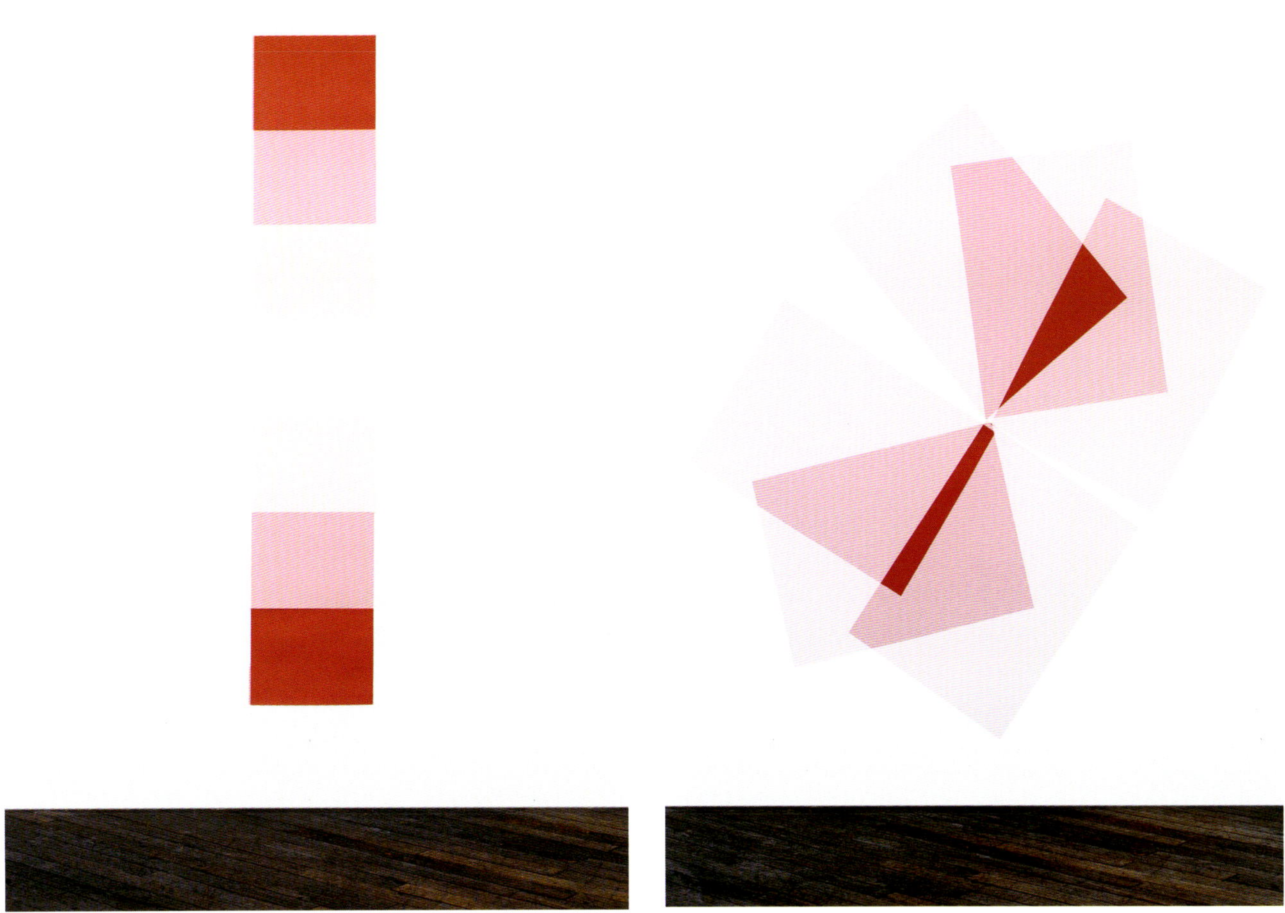

Sleight of Hand #59, 2013
Sleight of Hand #56, 2013

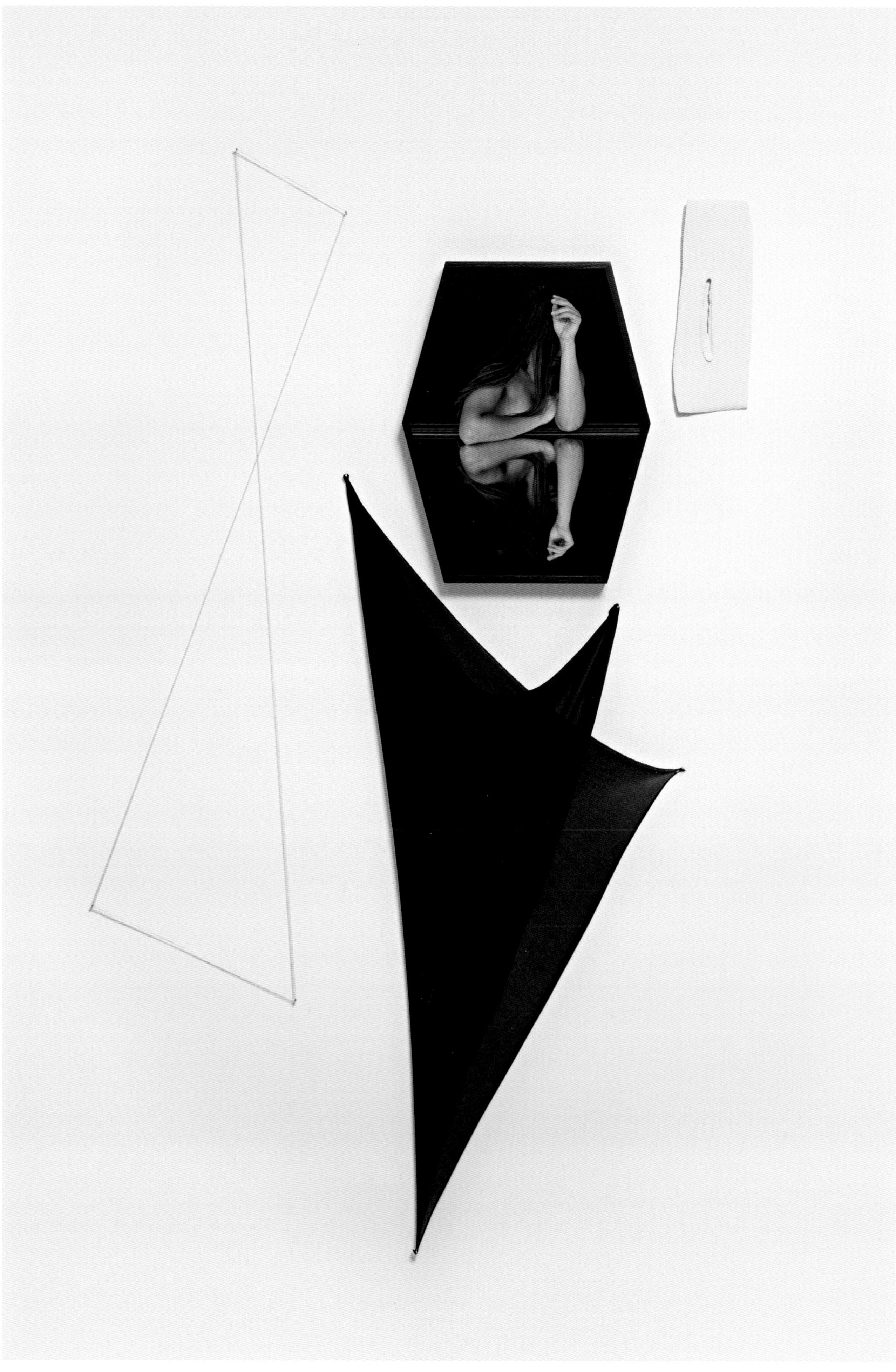

Material Gestures (Sister #1), 2012

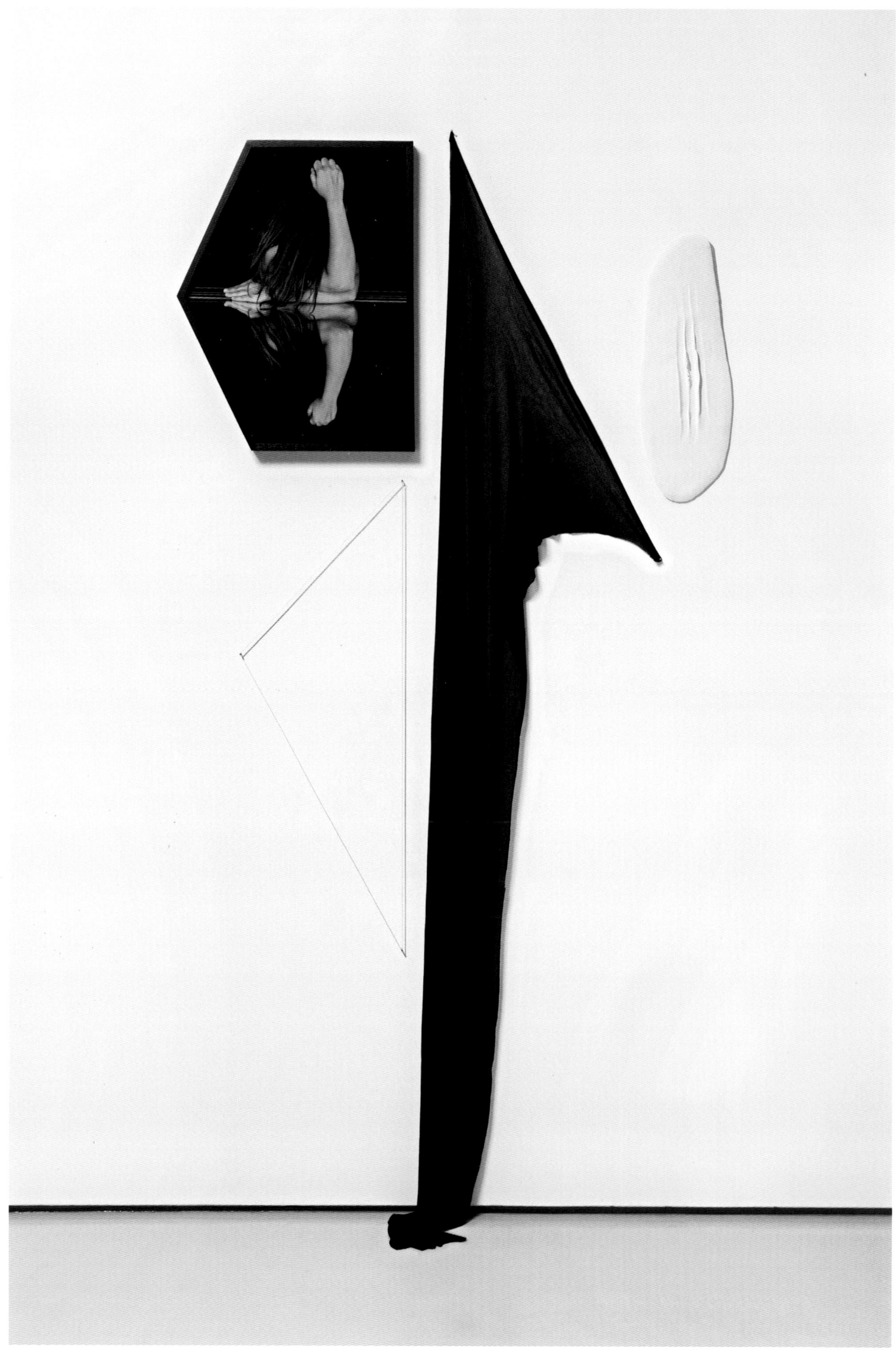

Material Gestures (Sister #2), 2012

Paige Sweet

Feminine. As soon as I think the word in relation to Sheree Hovsepian's work, I pause to wonder what I mean by it. But every word I reach for diffracts to a dissimilar word—delicacy is matched with solidity, firmness diverted by softness, intimacy detoured to distance. I begin to think that the hard lines and geometrical shapes conventionally associated with modernism give Hovsepian's work an equally masculine aspect. Perhaps this is the first invitation of her work: to dwell in a layering of masculine and feminine associations, to rethink their relation or, perhaps, to open up new relations, especially as pertains to the body and desire.

The symbolic tendencies I am describing as feminine and masculine in Hovsepian's work refuse opposition, but this only becomes evident when one lingers. This is, perhaps the second invitation: to linger. Only when we linger can we discern how the *presentation* of any given piece becomes meaningful only when its *process* unfolds. What appears in presentation often seems to bend away from its process—that is, constraint and control seem to rule presentation, whereas the process is all about experimentation and risk of failure. This asymmetrical relation between presentation and process is not only indicative of the highly conceptual nature of Hovsepian's work, but is also endemic to the way the body and desire are set and reset into forms to transform the relations between masculine and feminine aspects.

Lucida, for example, like many pieces from the *Velvet Assemblage Works* series (2019–2023) (such as *Euclidean Space*, *Acolyte*, and *Empath*; p. 2, 5, 6, 18), imparts a sense of control in the way the objects are precisely balanced in relation to one another. But if control were so certain, there would be no need for repetition. The precariousness attendant to the processes of making—the risk of ceramic breakage, the uncertainty of photographic exposure—is repeated across the objects, simultaneously emphasizing their fragility, and bracing against it. The repetition of forms asks what a half-moon ceramic shape says to a body fragmented to match, how the curved rigidity of a ceramic semi-circle communicates with the vulnerability of a bent back, or what spinal strength means as it releases into forward folding lunules. The fragment of a body always leaves one wanting more—a desire that is conjured and held taut in these works as a question of the body and what it can mean.

Across the various assemblages, the body is diagramed and articulated as a set of relations to objects, but the works also reframe the body from the gaze of these objects. The body is alternately centered and decentered, mimicking crescent forms or else reaching and bending away toward other unseen objects. The lines of desire articulated among objects is conveyed through the string, which alternatively and ambivalently connects, ignores, refracts, balances, and grids the various elements in any given piece. The string communicates how desire crosses the body to join it to other objects.

Many feminists have observed the way that absence, lack, and "darkness" have structured and limited conceptualizations of the feminine in Western metaphysics. The mostly black palette of Hovsepian's work recalls feminist practitioners like Louise Bourgeois (1911–2010), Hélène Cixous (b. 1937), and Kathy Acker (1947–1997), all of whom show that there is much to be gained by playing in or with darkness, which illuminates a different logic. These practitioners advance a notion of the feminine that eschews silence, distortion, and repression. In short, the feminine as feminist project declines to think the feminine as negation of the masculine. Instead, these practitioners shape the feminine in relation to experimental syntax, libidinal rearrangements, uncharted geographies of desire, and reimagined bodies. They resurrect unconscious dimensions of the feminine to engender new meanings. Hovsepian joins this chorus by showing how the intimate relation between presentation and process calls on us to hold together apparent oppositions— like presence and absence, masculine and feminine, control and vulnerability— to attend to their intricate intertwinement.

To hold together process and presentation in the way I am suggesting is an enticement to reflect on how the pulsing presence of unconscious dynamics make themselves knowable in conscious life. In this sense, we might see echoes of Kathy Acker's "Dream Maps"[1] and the bodily ego as rendered in Bourgeois' sculptures and drawings when we look at the geometric shapes and unlikely juxtaposition of objects in Hovsepian's assemblages. Her work differs from Acker's and Bourgeois' in the way it tenuously contains mess and breakdown within the process. And yet, it has in common with the novelist and the artist an intimate relation to the body where the relays of desire continually strive to map out new relations, where the unruliness of the unconscious always threatens the order and logic of consciousness.

Another articulation of this dynamic can be found in Cixous' call for an *écriture féminine*, a feminine writing that unleashes unconscious libidinal drives to generate new forms of being. A third invitation of Hovsepian's work is perhaps to consider how the response to this call need not be confined to writing, as it is for Cixous. Indeed, a *création feminine,* a feminine making, may remain more faithful to the Imaginary given its associations with images, repetition, and the feminine.[2] Just as Cixous urges us to attend to the ways that the Imaginary transforms the Symbolic through experimental uses of language—and Acker and Bourgeois engender forms for unseen forces—Hovsepian's work invites us to linger in surprising arrangements of objects to inquire about how they map or re-reroute desire.

Desire always evinces an unsteady, skipping relation. It thrives in the spaces between control and the loss of control, between presentation and process, among bodies and forms. It may just as easily, though, indicate a yearning for something that never existed, or something that is still coming into being. This is what the photograms of the *Haptic Wonders* series (2012; p. 51–53) convey in the way they index something that never really was. That is, the image presented on the paper is not a representation, it eludes the "that-has-been" that Roland Barthes famously describes as a key attribute of photography.[3] Similarly, feminist thinkers like Cixous and Luce Irigaray (b. 1930) have argued that the feminine has never truly existed because it has yet to be represented as anything other than negation of the masculine. The feminine as something that never really was—analogous to Hovsepian's photograms—resonates with the call to give shape to the desire for a feminine beyond masculine demarcations.

In different ways, *Haptic Wonders* and *Muscle Memory* (2022; p. 32–33) show how the bodily dimension of the process is refracted through the presentation. In *Haptic Wonders* the stunning shapes index the movement of a body in relation to other objects (scraps of paper and light, for example). The photograms are bent around uncertainty—there is no way to know in advance what image will surface when the paper is developed. Similarly, with *Muscle Memory*, the figures presented show the effect of moving the body around a spot of ink. These works are not about *representing* the body, but rather present bodily movements as relations.

1   See Kathy Acker, *Blood and Guts in High School*, Grove Press, New York 1978, p. 46–51.

2   Like Cixous, I am borrowing Jacques Lacan's psychoanalytic concepts of the Symbolic and the Imaginary. Lacan describes the Symbolic as symbolically associated with the masculine, the phallic, law and order, and language, and the Imaginary as associated with the feminine, the maternal, mirroring and alienation, and images. We can pressure these distinctions, however, by observing that the Imaginary is not only the realm wherein one constantly recognizes and misrecognizes the self through the gaze of others, but is also a potent site for forming and reforming the libidinal relations that infuse meanings of the self in relation to others. See Jacques Lacan, *Écrits: A Selection*, trans. Alan Sheridan, Norton, New York 1977.

3   Roland Barthes, *Camera Lucida*, trans. Richard Howard, Hill and Wang, New York 1981, p. 77.

The ink becomes the memory of a body in motion, the circulation of desire from one object to another: ink to paper, muscle to marking, the body drawn into new forms. Across these works, the body moves according to laws of desire that are barely perceptible in the finished work.

If it is true that there is a set of associations between process, unconscious dynamics, and the feminine on the one hand, and presentation, consciousness, and masculinity on the other, this is not to suggest any rigid organization of meaning about art, psychical economies, or gender. On the contrary, it is to emphasize their entanglement. Even more: it is to emphasize how that process (the unconscious, the feminine) endures in presentation (consciousness, the masculine) in ways that are often overlooked, neglected, dismissed. In short, the feminine is felt, experienced, perceived if you know how to look. As Hovsepian's practice shows, the feminine is interwoven with the masculine in the same way that the process suffuses presentation. Setting the body into relation with new forms of desire that draws resources from masculine and feminine psychical dispositions—this is the feminist impulse infusing Hovsepian's work.

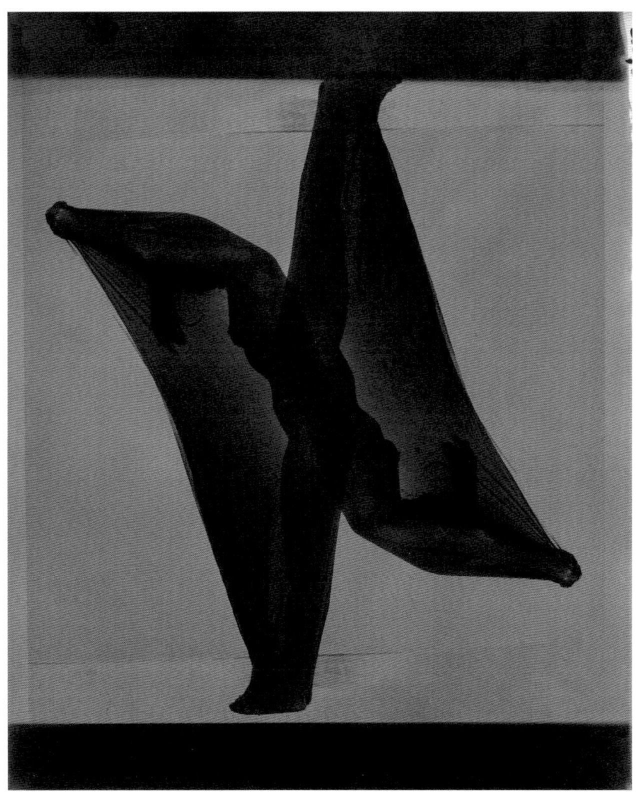

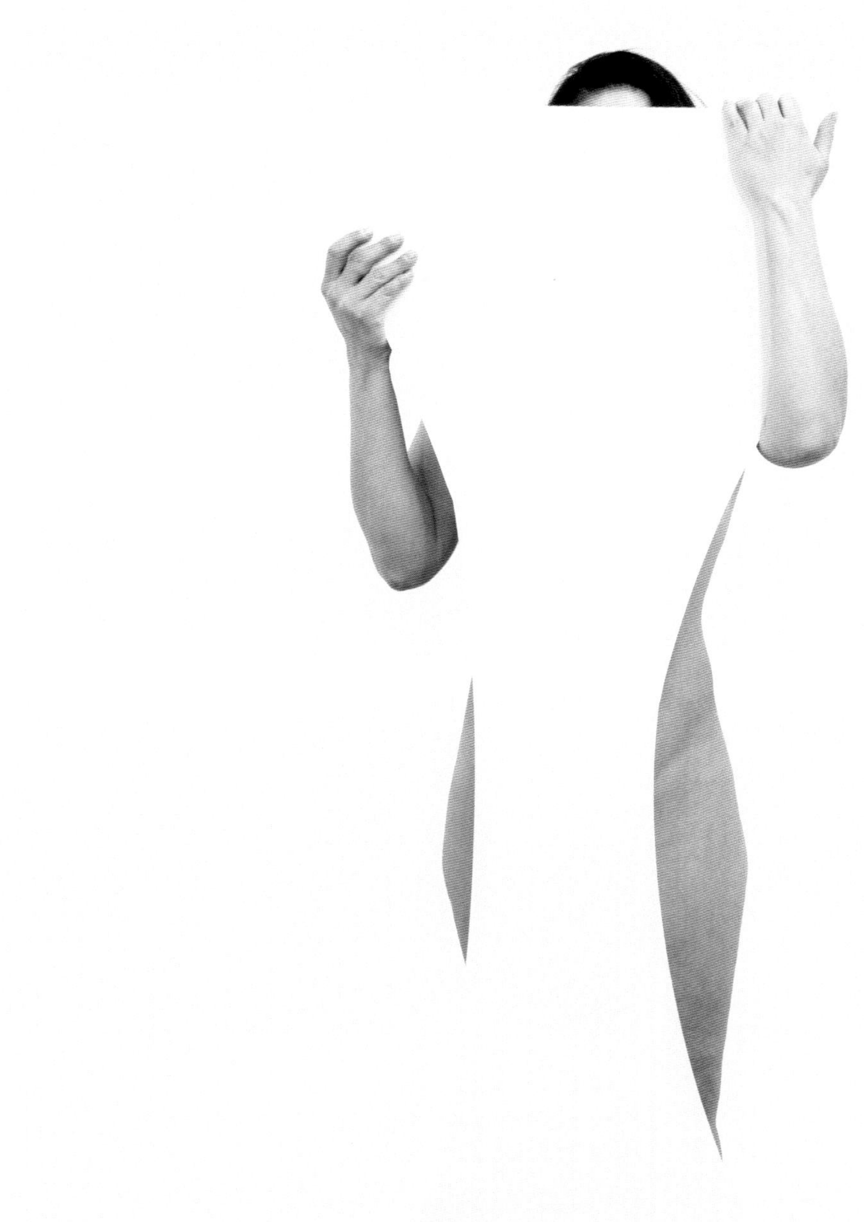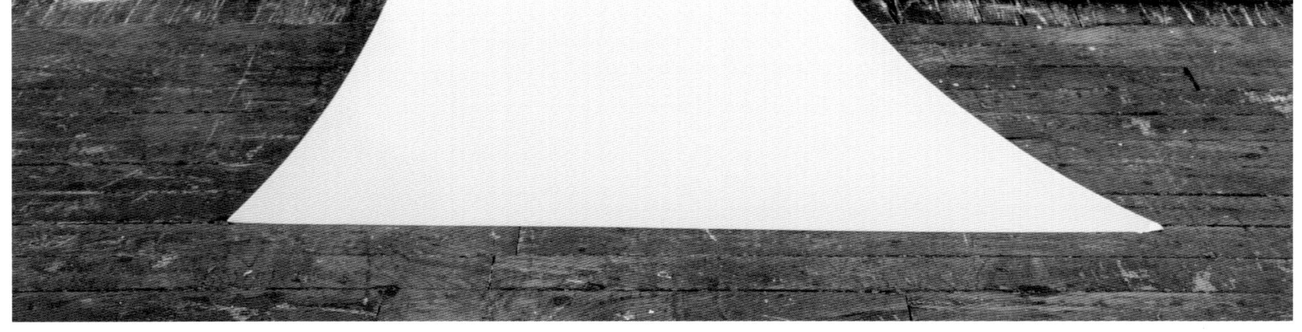

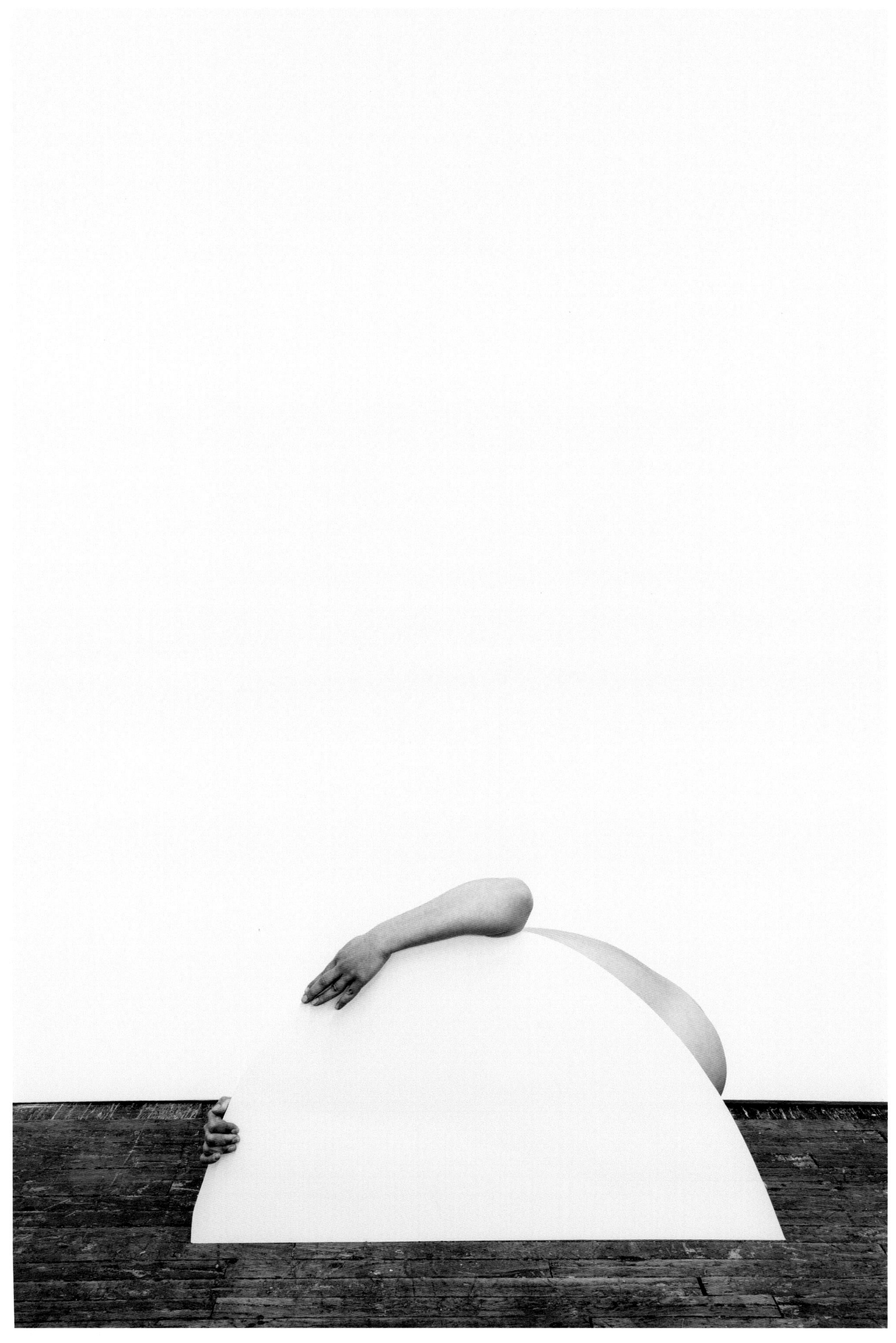

Leaning 1, 2019

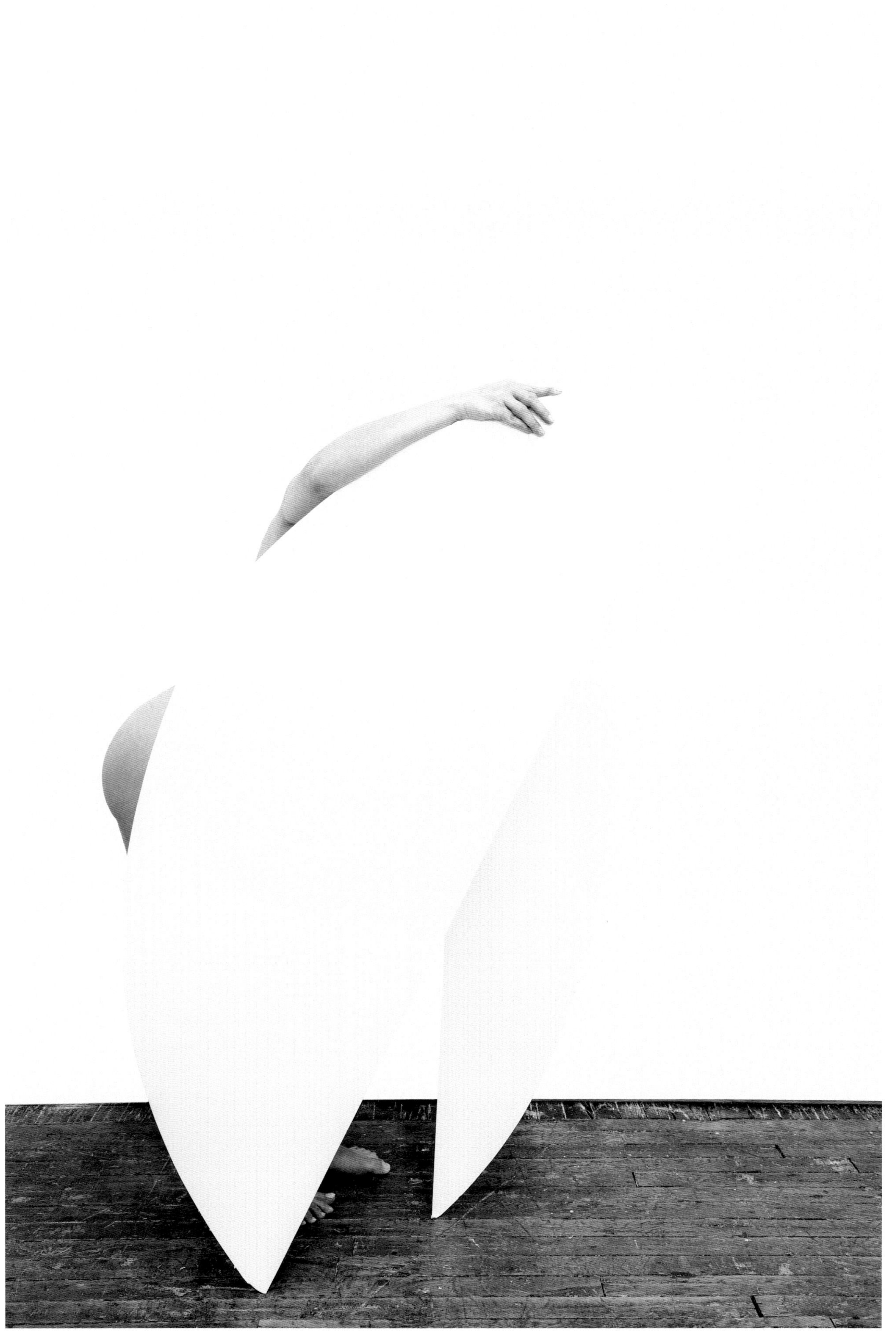

Leaning 5, 2019

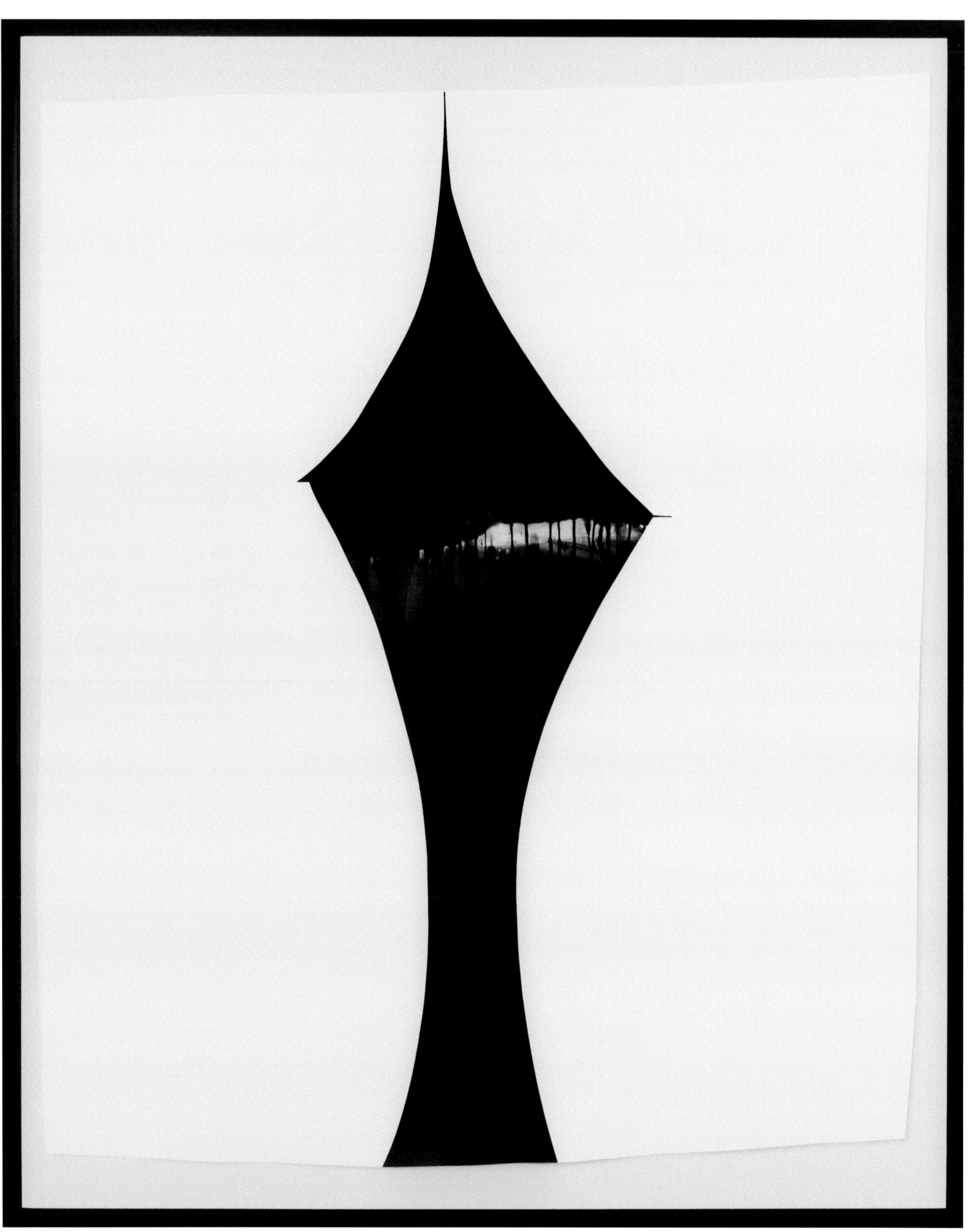

Even a Small Lighter Can Burn a Bridge, 2013

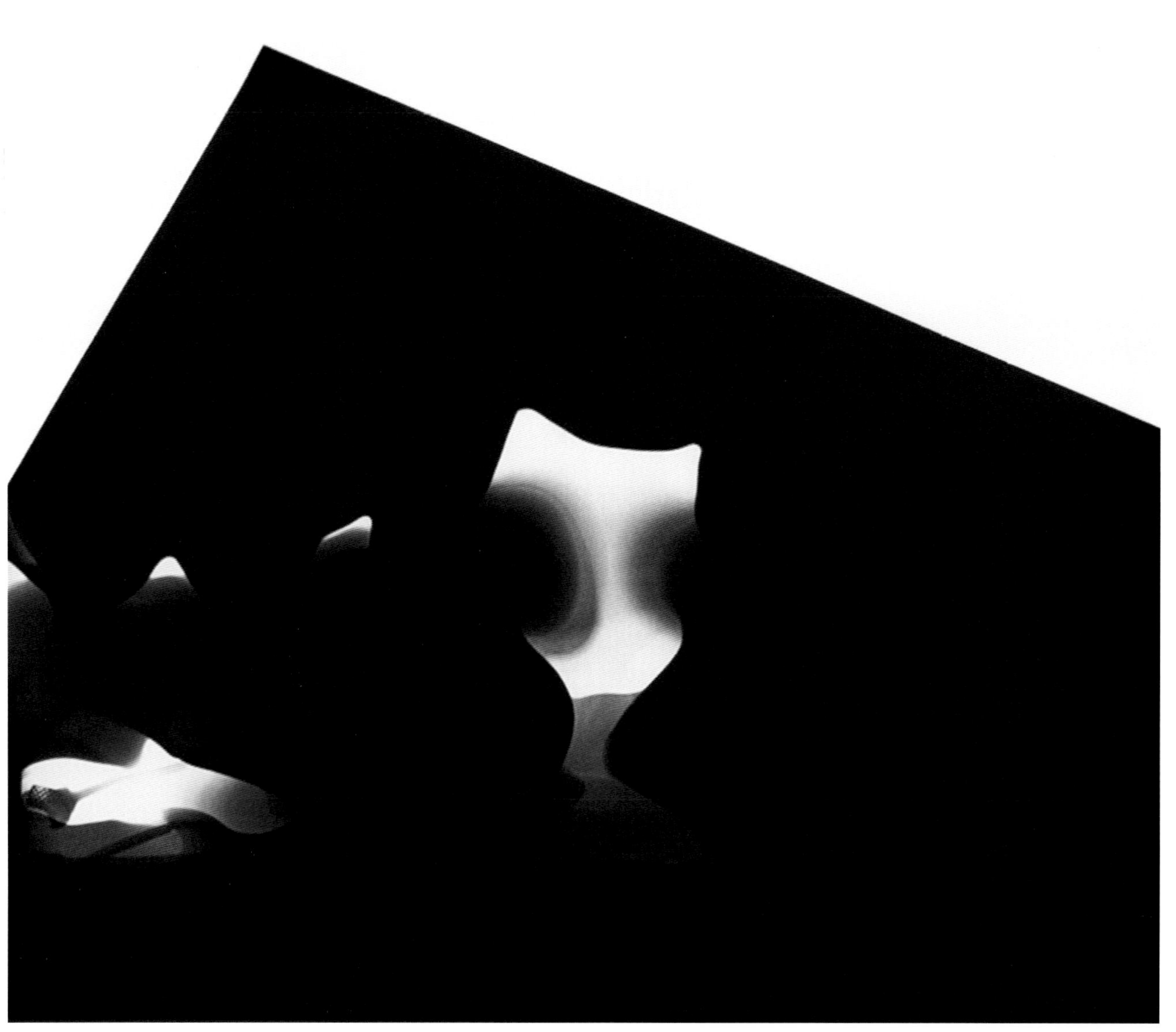

Untitled #92, *Haptic Wonders* series, 2012

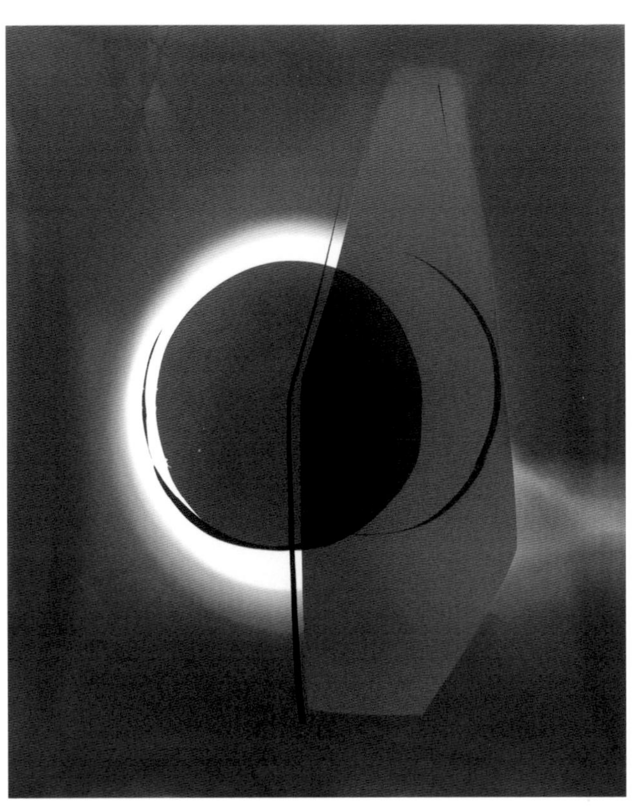

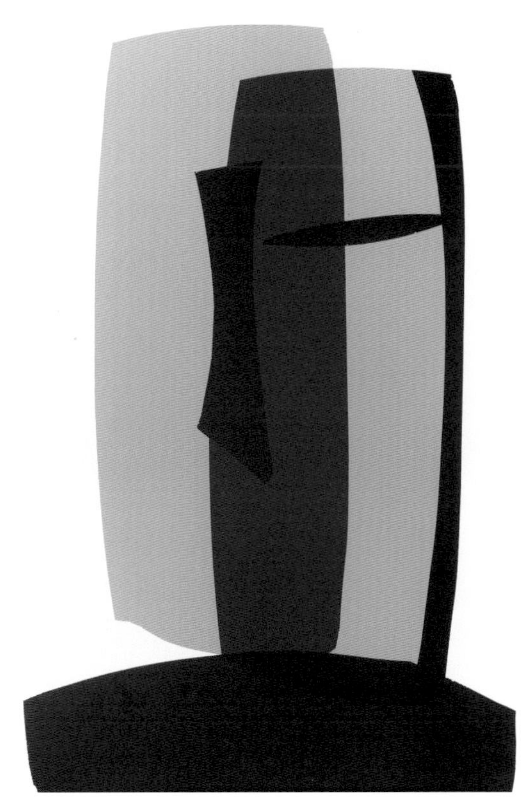

Untitled #80, *Haptic Wonders* series, 2012
Untitled #43, *Haptic Wonders* series, 2012

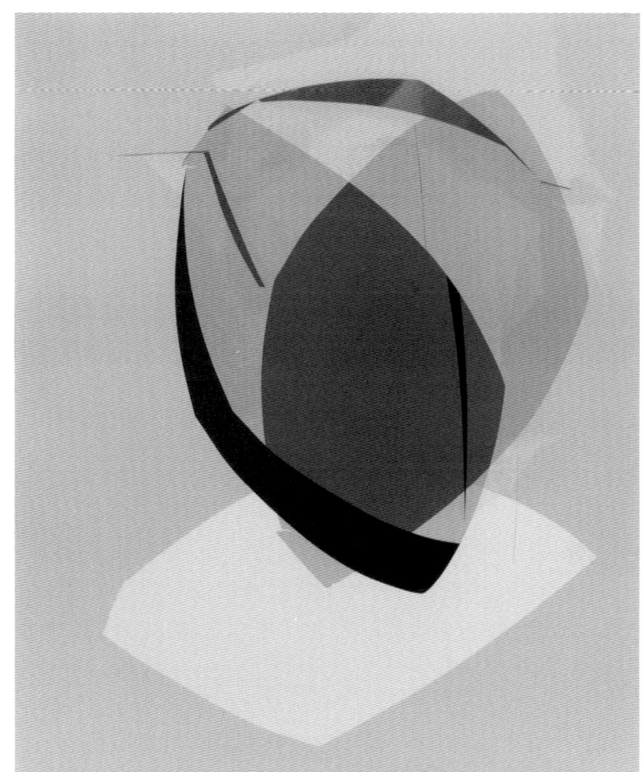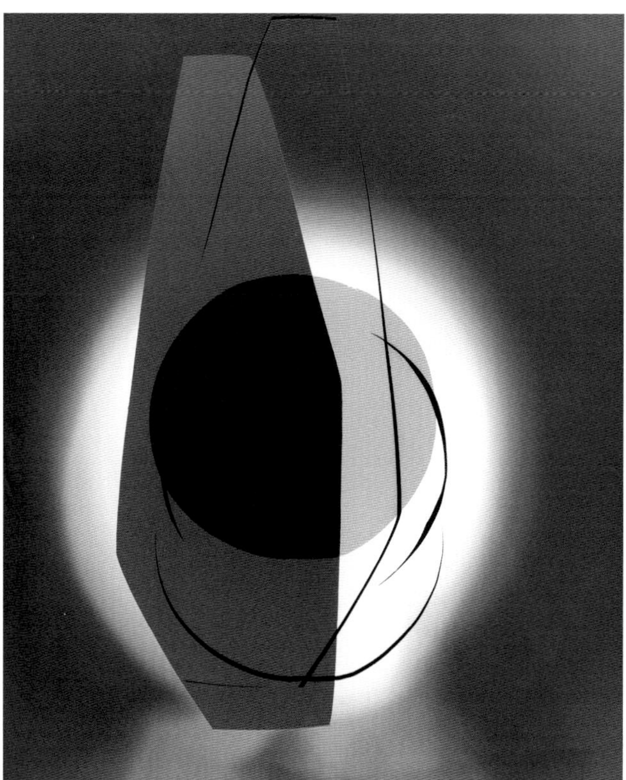

Untitled #20, Haptic Wonders series, 2012
Untitled #85, Haptic Wonders series, 2012

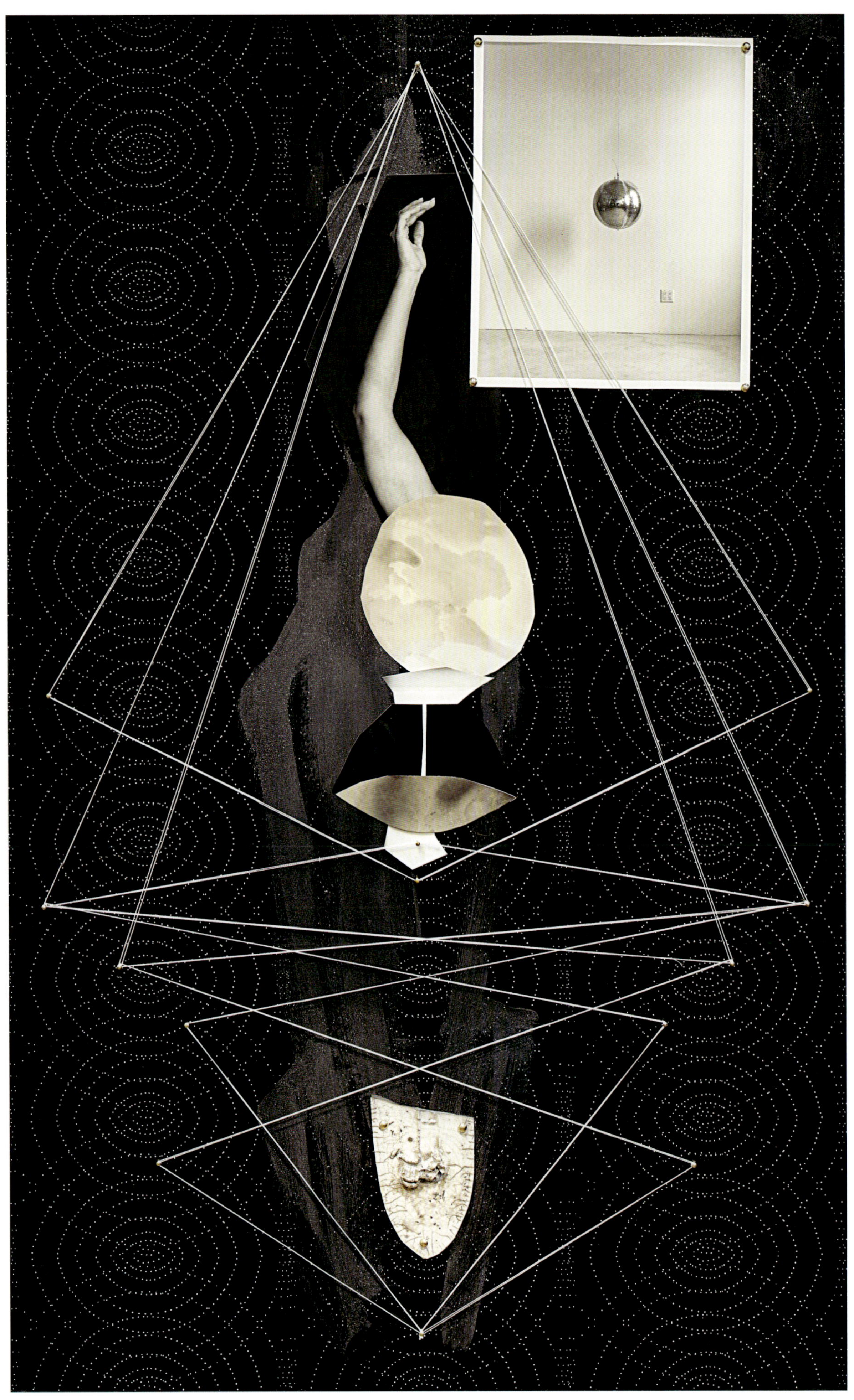

Lady, 2016

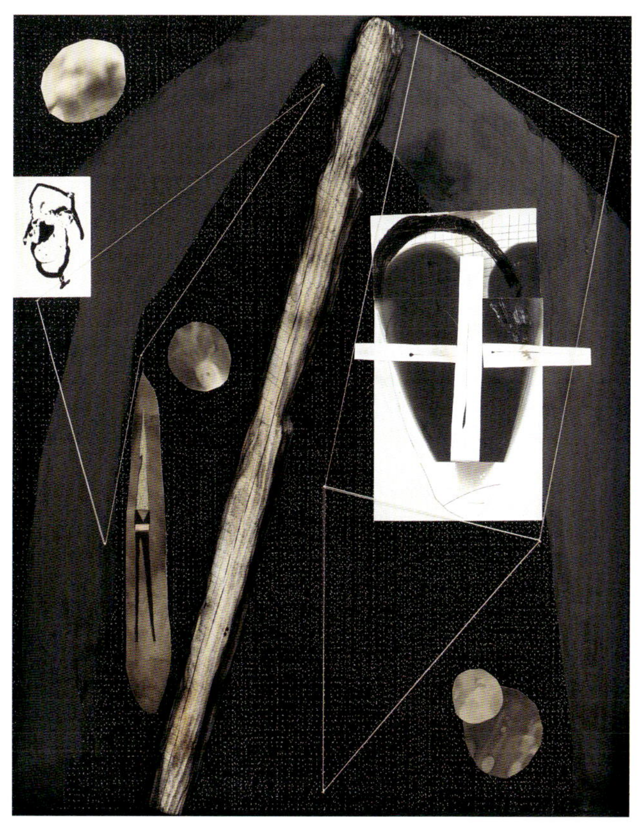

Reveries of a Solitary Walker, 2015

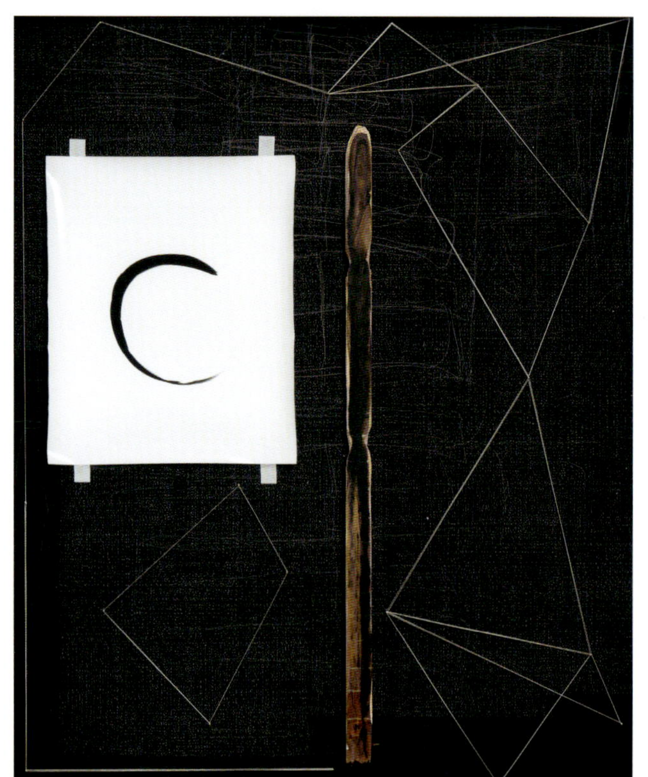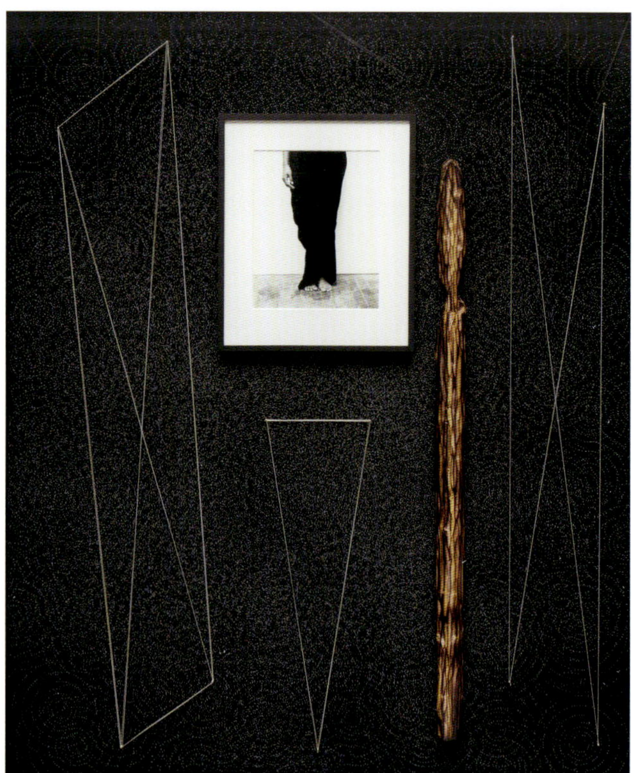

Honey Trap, 2014
Autobiographical Time Travel, 2015

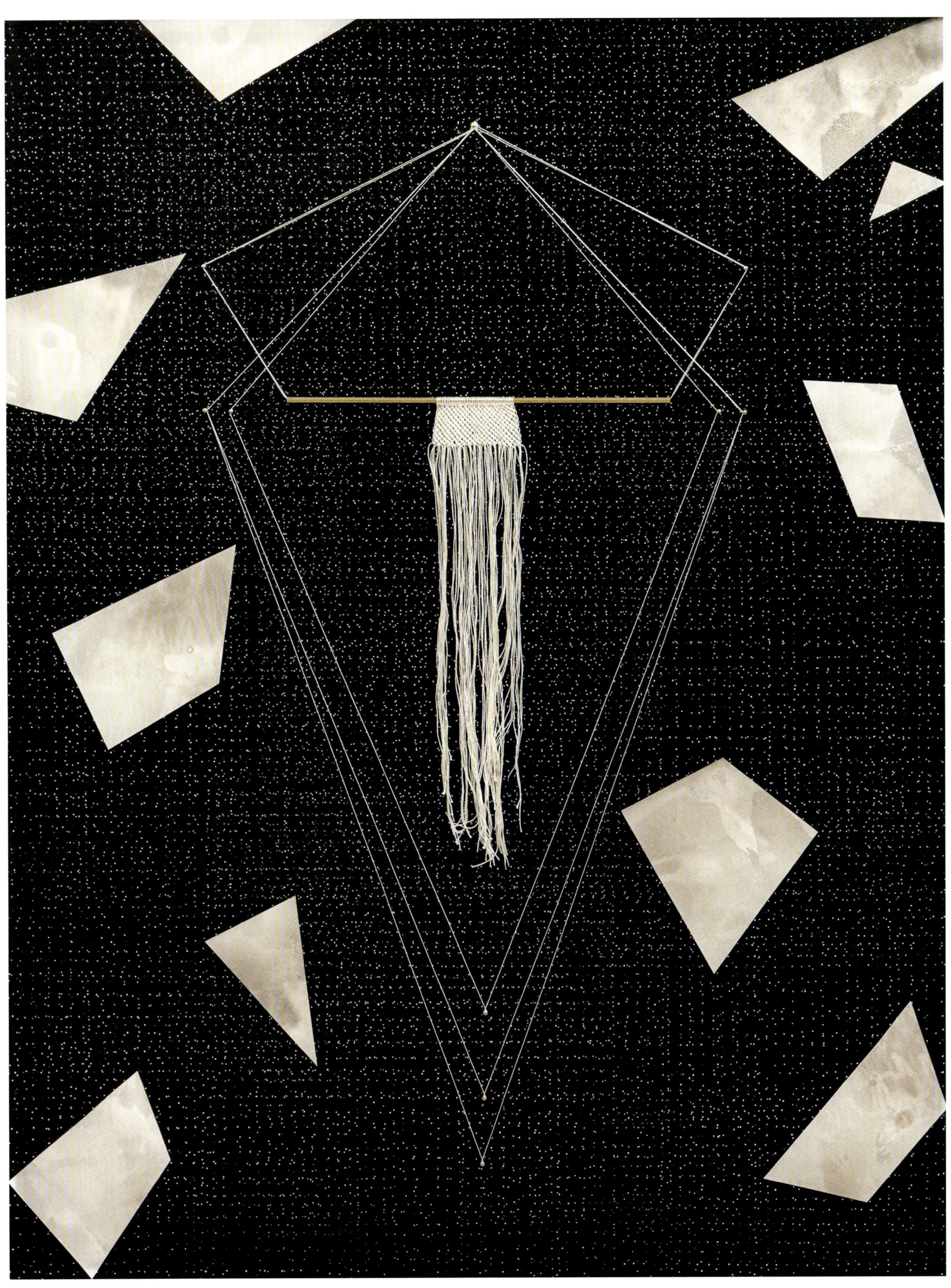

A Room of One's Own, 2014
→ *The Altogether*, Monique Meloche Gallery, Chicago, 2018

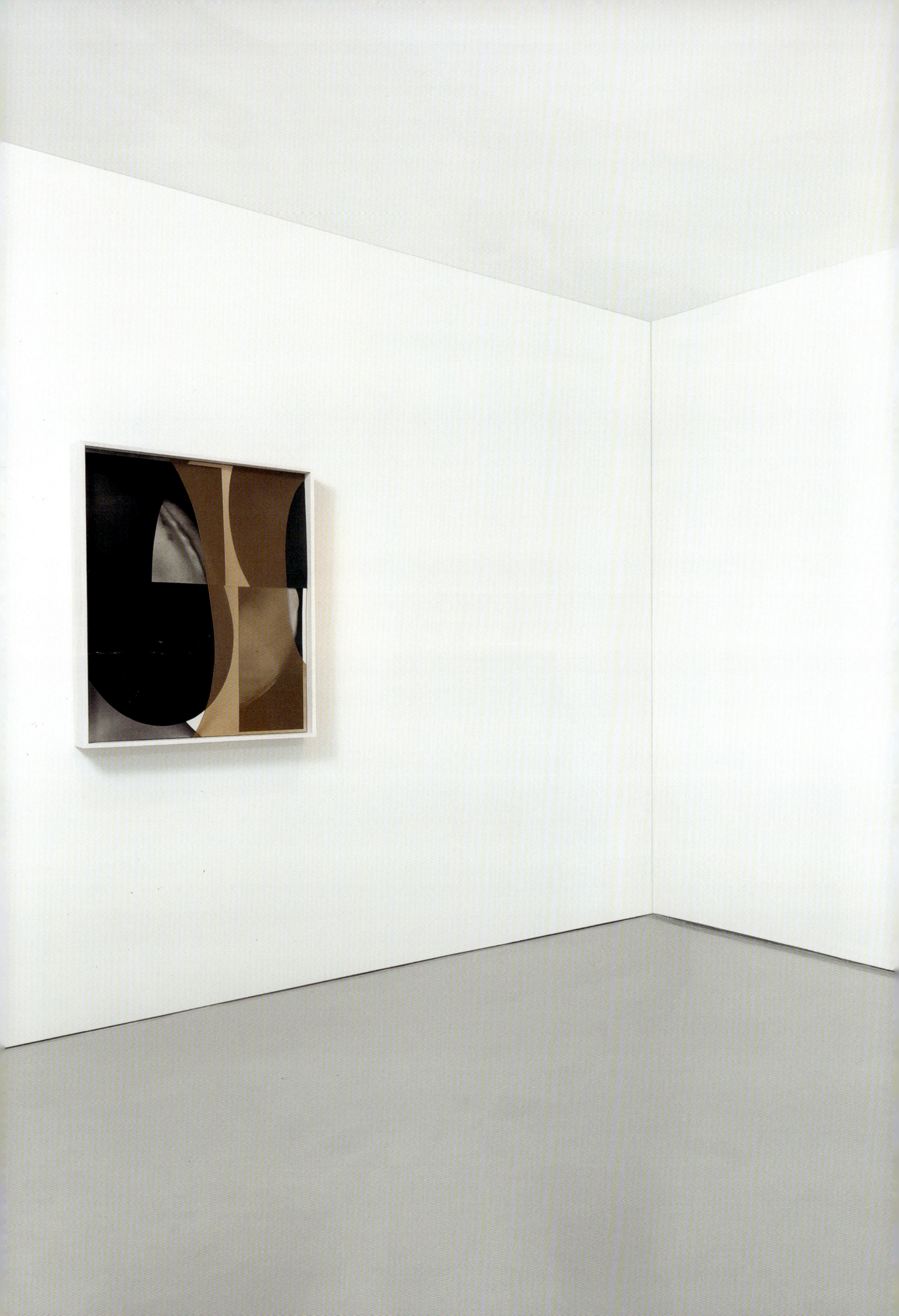

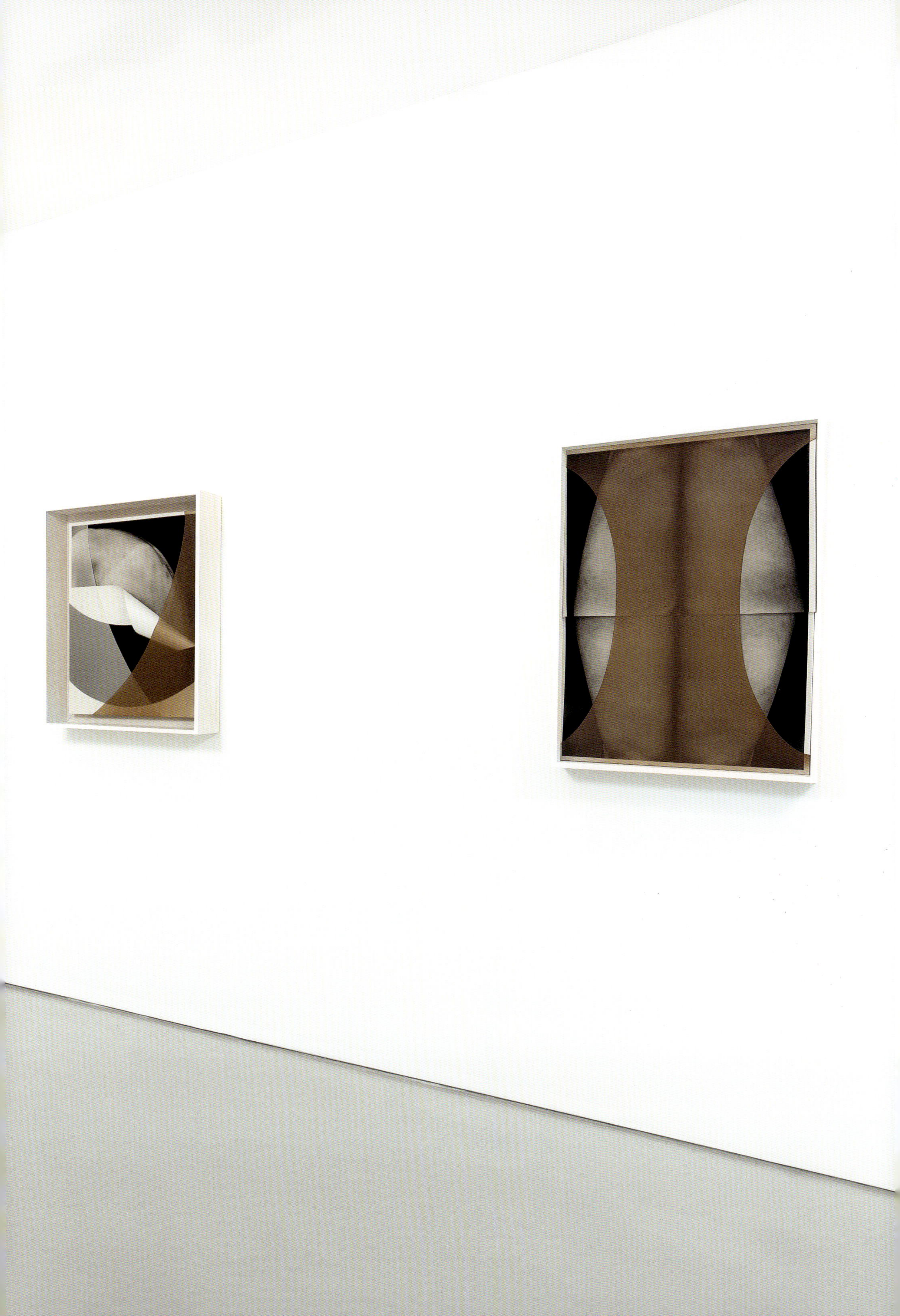

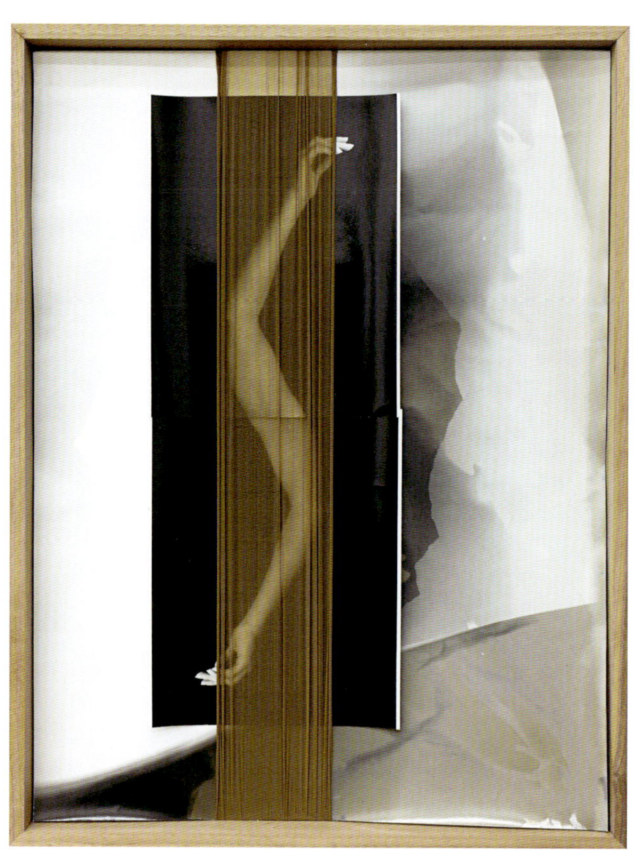

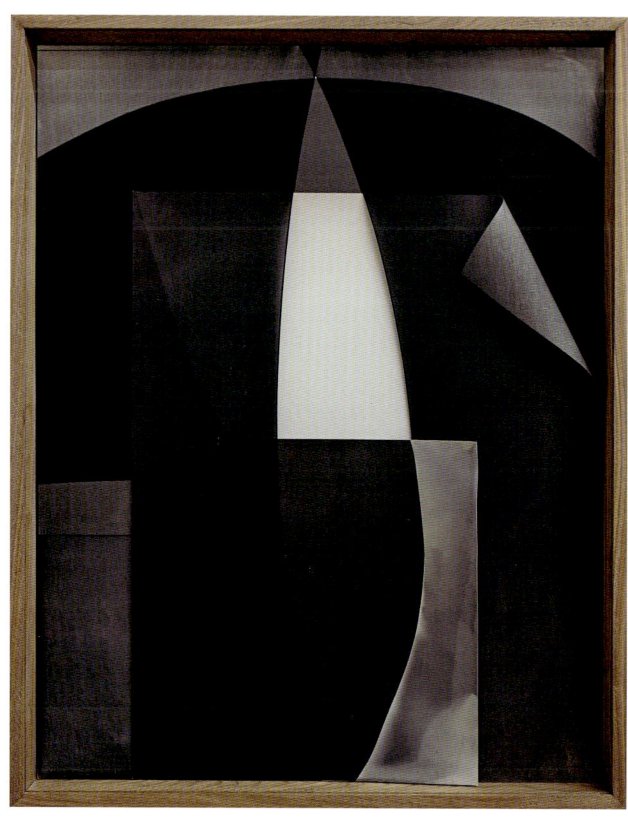

Beyond the Bounds, 2017
Inner Gaze, 2017

[p. 2, 5–20]
All works: *Velvet Assemblage Works*
series, 2020–2023

[p. 2]
Lucida, 2020
Silver gelatin print, ceramic, string,
nails, velvet in walnut artist's frame,
17.5 × 13.5 × 3.5 in. /
44.45 × 34.29 × 8.89 cm
Private collection

[p. 5]
Euclidean Space, 2022
Silver gelatin print, wood, string,
nails, velvet in walnut artist's
frame, 31.5 × 25.5 × 3.5 in. /
80.01 × 64.77 × 8.89 cm
Private collection

[p. 6]
Acolyte, 2023
Silver gelatin prints, ceramic, string,
nails, and velvet in walnut artist's
frame, 41.5 × 31.5 × 3.75 in. /
105.41 × 80.01 × 9.53 cm
Private collection

Relic, 2022
Silver gelatin print, ceramic, string,
nails, velvet in walnut artist's frame,
31.5 × 21.5 × 3.5 in. /
80.01 × 54.61 × 8.89 cm
Private collection

[p. 7]
Votary, 2023
Silver gelatin prints, wood, string,
nails, velvet in walnut artist's frame,
17.5 × 13.5 × 3.5 in. /
44.45 × 34.29 × 8.89 cm
Private collection

Cultured Pearl, 2021
Silver gelatin print, ceramic, string,
nails, velvet in walnut artist's frame,
17.5 × 13.5 × 3.5 in. /
44.45 × 34.29 × 8.89 cm
Private collection

[p. 8–9]
Exhibition view, *The Milk of Dreams*,
59th International Art Exhibition,
Venice, 2022

[p. 10]
Magical Thinking, 2021
Silver gelatin prints, wood, string,
nails, velvet in walnut artist's frame,
37.5 × 19.5 × 3.5 in. /
95.25 × 49.53 × 8.89 cm
Private collection

[p. 11]
Feedback, 2020
Silver gelatin prints, ceramic, nails,
velvet in walnut artist's frame,
17.25 × 13 × 3.5 in. /
43.81 × 33.02 × 8.89 cm
Private collection

[p. 12]
Cadence, 2022
Silver gelatin prints, ceramic, string,
nails, and velvet in walnut artist's
frame, 31.5 × 25.5 × 3.75 in. /
80.01 × 64.77 × 9.53 cm
Private collection

[p. 13]
Corporeal Nature, 2022
Silver gelatin print, ceramic, string,
nails, velvet in walnut artist's
frame, 31.5 × 25.5 × 3.5 in. /
80.01 × 64.77 × 8.89 cm
Aishti Foundation, Beirut

[p. 14]
Circle Pose, 2023
Silver gelatin prints, wood, string,
nails, and velvet in walnut artist's
frame, 31.5 × 25.5 × 3.5 in. /
80.01 × 64.77 × 8.89 cm
Private collection

Receiver, 2022
Silver gelatin prints, ceramic, string,
nails, and velvet in walnut artist's
frame, 31.5 × 25.5 × 3.75 in. /
80.01 × 64.77 × 9.53 cm
Private collection

[p. 15]
Radio, 2022
Silver gelatin prints, ceramic, wood,
nails, and velvet in walnut artist's
frame, 21.5 × 17.5 × 3.75 in. /
54.61 × 44.45 × 9.53 cm
Shah Garg Collection

Author, 2022
Silver gelatin prints, ceramic, string,
nails, and velvet in walnut artist's
frame, 31.5 × 25.5 × 3.5 in. /
80.01 × 64.77 × 8.89 cm
Private collection

[p. 16–17]
Exhibition view, *The Milk of Dreams*,
59th International Art Exhibition,
Venice, 2022

[p. 18]
Empath, 2019
Silver gelatin print, ceramic, string,
nails, velvet in walnut artist's frame,
17.5 × 13.5 × 3.5 in. /
44.45 × 34.29 × 8.89 cm
Private collection

Musing, 2020
Silver gelatin prints, string, nails,
velvet in walnut artist's frame,
17.25 × 13.5 × 3.5 in. /
43.81 × 34.29 × 8.89 cm
Private collection

[p. 19]
Parallel, 2022
Silver gelatin prints, ceramic, nails,
velvet in walnut artist's frame,
31.5 × 25.5 × 3.5 in. /
80.01 × 64.77 × 8.89 cm
Private collection

[p. 20]
Model, 2022
Silver gelatin prints, ceramic, wood,
string, nails, velvet in walnut artist's
frame, 41.5 × 31.5 × 3.75 in. /
105.41 × 80.01 × 9.53 cm
Private collection

[p. 22–26]
Contact sheets, 2012–2022

[p. 27]
As It Is, 2017
Archival dye transfer print, framed
silver gelatin print, acrylic, graphite,
found mask, macrame, string, nails,
bronze sculpture mounted on wood,
wood base, 90 × 50 × 16 in. /
228.60 × 127 × 40.64 cm
Private collection

[p. 28]
Kore, 2014
Bronze, wood base,
11 × 10.75 × 31 in. /
27.94 × 27.31 × 78.74 cm
Collection of the Park Hyatt New York

Proxy, 2014
Silver nitrate patina on bronze
with wood, 20 × 6 × 6 in. /
50.8 × 15.24 × 15.24 cm
Private collection

[p. 29]
Exhibition view, *Domes*, Bischoff/
Weiss Gallery, London, 2013

[p. 30–31]
Exhibition view, *Leaning In*, Rachel
Uffner Gallery, New York, 2022

[p. 32]
Untitled #2, *Muscle Memory* series,
2022
Ink and oil on paper in white
maple frame, 73 × 56.5 × 2.25 in. /
185.42 × 143.51 × 5.72 cm
Manuela & Iwan Wirth Collection

[p. 33]
Untitled #1, *Muscle Memory* series,
2022
Ink and oil on paper in white
maple frame, 73 × 56.5 × 2.25 in. /
185.42 × 143.51 × 5.72 cm
Private collection

[p. 34]
Sleight of Hand #78, 2013
C-print, 40 × 30 in. /
101.60 × 76.20 cm
Private collection

[p. 35]
Sleight of Hand #71, 2013
C-print, 40 × 30 in. /
101.60 × 76.20 cm
Private collection

[p. 36–37]
Exhibition view, *Domes*, Bischoff/
Weiss Gallery, London, 2013

[p. 38]
Sleight of Hand #4, 2013
C-print, 40 × 30 in. /
101.60 × 76.20 cm
Private collection

Sleight of Hand #5, 2013
C-print, 40 × 30 in. /
101.60 × 76.20 cm
Private collection

[p. 39]
Sleight of Hand #59, 2013
C-print, 40 × 30 in. /
101.60 × 76.20 cm
Private collection

Sleight of Hand #56, 2013
C-print, 40 × 30 in. /
101.60 × 76.20 cm
Private collection

[p. 40]
Material Gestures (Sister #1), 2012
Silver gelatin print, fabric, string,
nails, and porcelain,
72 × 48 in. / 182.88 × 121.92 cm
Private collection

[p. 41]
*Material Gestures (A Moment
in Latency)*, 2016
Fabric, unique silver gelatin photogram, drawing paper, and pins,
50 × 86 in. / 127 × 218.44 cm
Artist's Collection

[p. 42]
Material Gestures (Sister #2), 2012
Silver gelatin print, fabric, string,
nails, and porcelain,
74 × 40 in. / 188 × 101.60 cm
Artist's Collection

[p. 45]
The Form of Things V, 2017
Unique gelatinized silver gelatin
print, 21 × 17 in. / 53.34 × 43.18 cm
Artist's Collection

[p. 47]
Leaning 3, 2019
Silver gelatin print,
24 × 16 in. / 60.96 × 40.64 cm
Private collection

[p. 48]
Leaning 1, 2019
Silver gelatin print,
40 × 27 in. / 101.60 × 68.58 cm
Private collection

[p. 49]
Leaning 5, 2019
Silver gelatin print,
40 × 27 in. / 101.60 × 68.58 cm
Private collection

[p. 50]
*Even a Small Lighter Can Burn
a Bridge*, 2013
Unique silver gelatin photogram,
50 × 40 in. / 127 × 101.60 cm
Artist's Collection

[p. 51]
Untitled #92, *Haptic Wonders*
series, 2012
Unique gelatin silver photogram,
24 × 20 in. / 60.96 × 50.80 cm
Artist's Collection

[p. 52]
Untitled #80, *Haptic Wonders*
series, 2012
Unique gelatin silver photogram,
24 × 20 in. / 60.96 × 50.80 cm
Private collection

Untitled #43, *Haptic Wonders*
series, 2012
Unique gelatin silver photogram,
24 × 20 in. / 60.96 × 50.80 cm
Artist's Collection

[p. 53]
Untitled #20, *Haptic Wonders*
series, 2012
Unique gelatin silver photogram,
20.5 × 17 in. / 52.07 × 43.18 cm
Private collection

Untitled #85, *Haptic Wonders*
series, 2012
Unique gelatin silver photogram,
24 × 20 in. / 60.96 × 50.80 cm
Artist's Collection

[p. 54]
Lady, 2016
Archival dye transfer print, silver
gelatin print, Raku fired porcelain,
string, brass nails,
26 × 40 in. / 66.04 × 101.60 cm
Artist's Collection

[p. 55]
Reveries of a Solitary Walker, 2015
Archival dye transfer print, graphite,
acrylic, silver gelatin prints, wood,
ink drawing on paper, brass nails,
and string, 51 × 41 × 2 1/2 in. /
129.54 × 104.14 × 6.35 cm
Artist's Collection

[p. 56]
Honey Trap, 2014
Archival dye transfer print, unique
silver gelatin photogram, graphite,
wood, tape, string and nails,
30 × 40 in. / 76.20 × 101.60 cm
Private collection

Autobiographical Time Travel, 2015
Archival dye transfer print, framed
silver gelatin print, wood, string,
brass nails, graphite and acrylic,
50 × 60 in. / 127 × 152.40 cm
Artist's Collection

[p. 57]
A Room of One's Own, 2014
Archival dye transfer print, silver
gelatin photogram, graphite,
string, bronze, and nails,
30 × 40 in. / 76.20 × 101.60 cm
Artist's Collection

[p. 58–59]
Exhibition view, *The Altogether*,
Monique Meloche Gallery, Chicago,
2018

[p. 60]
Beyond the Bounds, 2017
Silver gelatin photographs, silver
gelatin photograms, nylon in walnut
artist's frame, 25 × 19 × 2.5 in. /
63.50 × 48.26 × 6.35 cm
Private collection

Inner Gaze, 2017
Silver gelatin photographs, silver
gelatin photograms, nylon in walnut
artist's frame, 31 × 21 × 4 in. /
78.74 × 53.34 × 10.16 cm
Artist's Collection

[p. 64]
Floor Work, 2017
Silver gelatin photographs and
graphite on paper mounted on wood,
nylon fabric, acrylic, brass nails,
walnut artist's frame, 19 × 13.5 × 2 in. /
48.26 × 34.29 × 5.08 cm
Private collection

Born in 1974 in Isfahan, Iran,
Sheree Hovsepian lives in New York.

She received her MFA from
the School of the Art Institute
of Chicago in 2002.
She is represented by Rachel
Uffner Gallery, New York.

Solo Exhibitions (Selection)

2025
Figure Ground,
Rachel Uffner Gallery, New York

2022
Leaning In, Rachel Uffner Gallery,
New York

2020
Musing, Halsey McKay Gallery,
East Hampton

2019
Higher Pictures Gallery, New York
*Sheree Hovsepian and Paul
Mpagi Sepuya*, Team Bungalow,
Los Angeles

2018
The Altogether, Monique Meloche
Gallery, Chicago

2017
Halsey McKay Gallery, East Hampton
Higher Pictures Gallery, New York

2015
Reveries of a Solitary Walker,
Monique Meloche Gallery, Chicago

2014
Soft Landing, Gallery 44–Centre for
Contemporary Photography, Toronto

2013
Domes, Bischoff/Weiss Gallery,
London

2011
Haptic Wonders, Monique Meloche
Gallery, Chicago

Group Exhibitions (Selection)

2025
*Synchronicities: Intersecting
Figuration with Abstraction*,
Bemis Center for Contemporary
Arts, Omaha (Nebraska)

2024
In and Out, Sidecar, Los Angeles
The Selves, Nicola Vassell Gallery,
New York
A Study in Form (Chapter Two),
James Fuentes Gallery, New York

2023
Artists Choose Parrish, Part II,
The Parrish Art Museum, Water Mill
The Nightingale and the Rose,
The Israel Museum, Jerusalem
Love Songs, International Center
of Photography, New York
Making their Mark, Shah Garg
Foundation, New York
WOMEN, Nicole Klagsbrun Gallery,
New York
*Direct Contact: Cameraless
Photography Now*, Sidney and Lois
Eskenazi Museum of Art Indiana
University, Bloomington (Indiana)

2022
The Milk of Dreams, 59th Biennale
di Venezia, Venice

2021
*Affinities for Abstraction: Women
Artists on Eastern Long Island,
1950–2020*, The Parrish Art
Museum, Water Mill
There's There There, Hauser & Wirth,
Southampton
Arches and Ink, Rachel Uffner
Gallery, New York

2020
A Show of Hands, September
Gallery, Hudson
*Never Done: 100 Years of Women
in Politics and Beyond*, Tang
Teaching Museum, Saratoga Springs

2019
Seductive Reduction, CHART
Gallery, New York
Vanishing Act, Halsey McKay
Gallery, East Hampton

2017
Where Do We Stand?, The Drawing
Center, New York
Material Gestures, Stony Island
Arts Bank, Chicago

Bibliography (Selection)

Simon Baker (ed.), *Love Songs: Photography and Intimacy*, International Center of Photography, exh. cat., DAP, New York 2023, p. 102–111
Yuvan Etgar (ed.), *Vitamin C+: Collage in Contemporary Art*, Phaidon, London 2023, p. 114–115
Randy Kennedy (ed.), "Artists and Sitters: Henry Taylor in Conversation with Sheree Hovsepian about Depiction and the Depicted," *Manuela Magazine*, no. 7, Winter 2022–2023, p. 42–54
Cecilia Alemani (ed.), *59th Venice Biennale: The Milk of Dreams*, exh. cat., La Biennale di Venezia, Venice 2022, p. 144–147
Xaviera Simmons, Phebe Wahl (eds.), *Art Basel Miami Beach Magazine*, DM Luxury, Miami, December 2021, p. 116–119
Charlotte Cotton, *The Photograph as Contemporary Art*, World of Art series, Thames & Hudson, London 2020, p. 297, 299
Haley Mellin. "Sheree Hovsepian, Artists on Artists," *Bomb Magazine*, no. 139, Spring 2017, p. 152–153
Christian Rattemeyer, "Sheree Hovsepian: Magic Matter," *Osmos Magazine*, no. 08, Spring 2016, p. 32–35
Alexis Dirks, Sheree Hovsepian, et al., *Reflections and Refractions*, Black Dog Press, London 2015, p. 40–50

Public Collections

Art Institute of Chicago, Chicago
Bronx Museum, New York
Komal Shah Collection, Atherton (California)
Northwestern Pritzker School of Law, Evanston (Illinois)
Solomon R. Guggenheim Museum, New York
Spertus Museum, Chicago
Studio Museum, Harlem
Zabludowicz Collection, London

Thank you to my husband Rashid Johnson whose love, support, and belief in my work give me the space to pursue my vision without hesitation. I am endlessly grateful for your insight, curiosity, and depth of thought.

To Julius, your presence has taught me that love is a force that stretches across past, present, and future, connecting generations in ways that transcend language. Through you both, I have encountered the depth and complexity of life in its purest form—an understanding that echoes in my work and in the way I move through the world.

I dedicate this book to my mother, Shahnaz Ghodsi-Hovsepian whose love and strength continue to resonate within me.
    Though she is no longer here, she remains a constant guide, her spirit present in every thread, every form, and every piece I bring into being.
—Sheree Hovsepian

Editorial Director
Clément Dirié

Editor
Elisa Nadel

Authors
Charlotte Cotton, Paige Sweet

Copy Editing and Proofreading
Clare Manchester

Graphic Design
Coline Houot

Typeface
Executive (www.optimo.ch)

Cover
Radio, 2022, details

Color Separation and Print
Musumeci S.p.A, Quart (Aosta)

Photo Credits
Ela Bialkowska/OKNO Studio: p. 8–9, 16–17; JSP Photography: cover, p. 5–7, 10–15, 18t, 19, 20, 30–33, 45; Courtesy Monique Meloche Gallery: p. 58–59; Object Studies: p. 41; Martin Parsekian: p. 2, 18b, 27, 28, 34, 35, 38–40, 42, 47–53, 60, 64; Plastiques: p. 29, 36–37; James Prinz: p. 54–57

Published by
JRP|Editions
Rue des Bains, 39
CH–1205 Geneva
www.jrp-editions.com

ISBN 978-3-03764-627-4

JRP|Editions publications are available internationally at selected bookstores and from the following distribution partners:

Austria, Germany, and Switzerland
Through JRP|Editions
books@jrp-editions.com

France
Les presses du réel
www.lespressesdureel.com

UK, other European countries, USA, Canada, Asia and Australia
ARTBOOK|D.A.P.
www.artbook.com

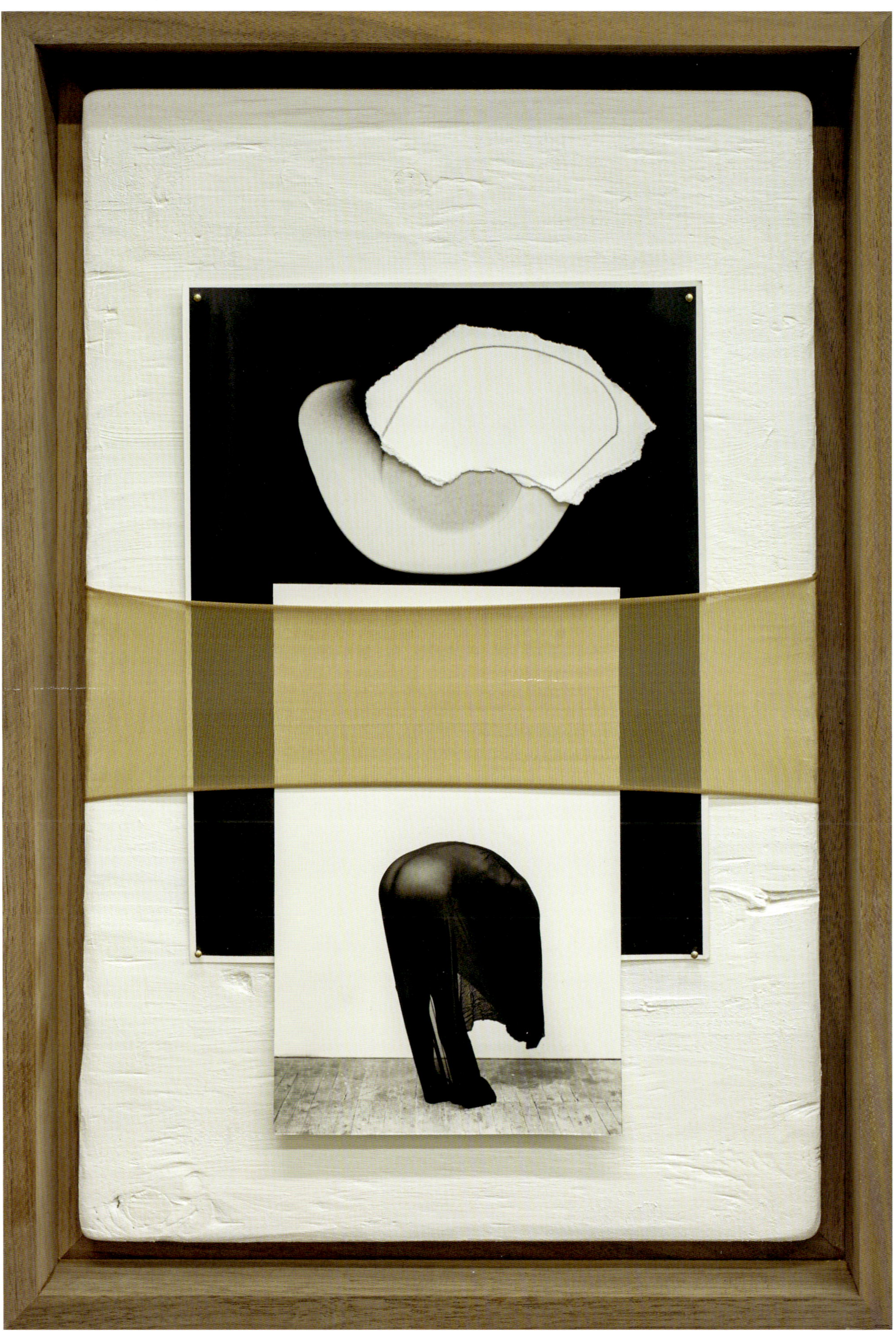

Floor Work, 2017